SEMINAR STUDIES IN HISTORY
The Thirty Years War

WITHDRAWN

SEMINAR STUDIES IN HISTORY
General Editor: Roger Lockyer

The Thirty Years War

Peter Limm

LONGMAN
London and New York

LONGMAN GROUP UK LIMITED
Longman House, Burnt Mill,
Harlow, Essex CM20 2JE, England
and Associated Companies throughout the World.

Published in the United States of America
by Longman Inc., New York

First published 1984
Third impression 1987
ISBN 0 582 35373 4

Set *in* 10/11 Linotron Baskerville

*Produced by Longman Group (FE) Ltd
Printed in Hong Kong*

British Library Cataloguing in Publication Data

Limm, Peter
  The Thirty Years War. — (Seminar studies in history)
  1. Thirty Years' War, 1618–1648
  I. Title   II. Series
  940.2'4   D258
  ISBN 0-582-35373-4

Library of Congress Cataloging in Publication Data

Limm, Peter
  The Thirty Years War.
  (Seminar studies in history)
  Bibliography: p.
  Includes index.
  1. Thirty Years' War, 1618–1648. I. Title. II. Series.
D258.L55 1984   940.2'4   83-27554
ISBN 0-582-35373-4

Contents

Contents

A note on currency

The exchange rates in contemporary Europe were roughly as follows:

4.8	thalers (or rixdollars)	
4.5	escudos	
12	livres tournois	to the £ sterling
10	Dutch florins	
6	Rhine florins	

Seminar Studies in History

Founding Editor: Patrick Richardson

Introduction

The Seminar Studies series was conceived by Patrick Richardson, whose experience of teaching history persuaded him of the need for something more substantial than a textbook chapter but less formidable than the specialised full-length academic work. He was also convinced that such studies, although limited in length, should provide an up-to-date and authoritative introduction to the topic under discussion as well as a selection of relevant documents and a comprehensive bibliography.

Patrick Richardson died in 1979, but by that time the Seminar Studies series was firmly established, and it continues to fulfil the rôle he intended for it. This book, like others in the series, is therefore a living tribute to a gifted and original teacher.

Note on the System of References:
A bold number in round brackets (**5**) in the text refers the reader to the corresponding entry in the Bibliography section at the end of the book. A bold number in square brackets, preceded by 'doc' [**doc. 6**] refers the reader to the corresponding items in the section of Documents, which follows the main text.

ROGER LOCKYER
General Editor

Sites associated with the Thirty Years War

Holy Roman Empire in 1648

Route of Gustavus Adolphus
1630–32

EKINGE

BALTIC SEA

Memel

Bornholm

Königsberg
Pillau
Danzig

PRUSSIA

KAMMIN

MERANIA
ettin

Vistula

Warsaw

POLAND

Oder

JSATIA
Steinau
AXONY

SILESIA

Friedland

Elbe
Glatz
Prague

OHEMIA
Jankow

MORAVIA

CARPATHIANS

AUSTRIA
anube
Vienna

Buda Pest

HUNGARY

Gratz

STYRIA
Drava

OTTOMAN EMPIRE

ARNIOLA

SLAVONIA
Danube

BOSNIA

Acknowledgements

We are grateful to the following for permission to reproduce copyright material:

Edward Arnold (Publishers) Ltd for extracts from *Sweden as a Great Power* by M. Roberts (ed.) and *Germany in the Thirty Years War* by G. Benecke ('Documents in Modern History' series); Macmillan, London and Basingstoke for extracts from *The Hapsburg and Hohenzollen Dynasties in the 17th and 18th Century* by C. A. Macartney (ed.); Macmillan Publishing Co. for an extract from pp. 291–293 *Renaissance and Reformation 1300–1648* (2nd Edition) by G. R. Elton (ed.) Copyright © 1968 by Macmillan Publishing Co.; University of Chicago Press for extracts from the article 'Military Revolution – A Myth?' by G. Parker in *Journal of Modern History* Vol. 48 (1976).

We have been unable to trace the copyright owners of *Readings in European History* by J. H. Robinson and would appreciate any information that would enable us to do so.

We are grateful to the following for permission to reproduce: map on pages viii–ix adapted from *Grosser Historischer Weltatlas*, vol. 3, Neuzeit, 4th edition (1981), Bayerischer Schulbuch-Verlag, Munich; map on page 39 from Taylor G. and Morris J.A: *A Sketchmap History of Britain and Europe 1485–1783*, Harrap; table from Astrom S.E., 'The Swedish Economy and Sweden's Role as a Great Power 1632–1697' in Roberts M: *Sweden's Age of Greatness 1632–1718*, Macmillan, 1973; table from Parker G., 'The Military Revolution – A Myth?' in *Journal of Modern History*, vol XLVIII, 1976, page 96, University of Chicago Press; table from G. Parker: *Europe in Crisis 1598–1648*, Fontana Paperbacks, 1979.

Cover: Gustavus Adolphus' prayer before the Battle of Lützen by Louis Braun. BBC Hulton Picture Library.

Part One: The Background, 1600–21

1 Areas of Conflict

One important feature of the period 1609–60 is the onset of total war in the years 1618 to 1628 and the historian is bound to be curious as to why it was that in the years before 1621 local European conflicts and military engagements could be limited to the initial belligerents and geographically contained, but that after that date they could not be. Why was it that for a good thirty years the local struggles of the European powers overlapped, intermingled and fought themselves to a weary standstill on the soil of the Holy Roman Empire and its border territories?

Western Europe

The main conflicts in western Europe centred around the struggle of the French monarchy and the United Provinces of the Netherlands against the two branches of the House of Habsburg, Spain and Austria. In the sixteenth century, Philip II of Spain had been committed to maintaining Catholic Christianity and Spain's prestige and security. The revolt of the Netherlands against Spanish policies (from 1566) and the failure of the Armada against England in 1588 merely served to strengthen Philip II's resolve to preserve the Spanish Imperial 'system' at all costs. In effect, Spain was forced to be permanently prepared for war.

After 1579, the southern provinces of the Netherlands – the 'Obedient Provinces' – once more agreed to recognise Spanish sovereignty and, from 1596, were governed by 'the Archdukes' Albert and Isabel. Philip II died in 1598, but Philip III continued to preserve Spain's interests in the world. Under the Archdukes the southern provinces of the Netherlands were re-Catholicised and a truce was arranged with the seven 'United Provinces' of the north (9 April 1609) to last for twelve years. However, Dutch statesmen foresaw that Spain would not easily abandon her claims to the northern provinces. At the outbreak of the rebellion, Spain had been the foremost maritime, commercial and colonial power in Europe, yet during the truce the United Provinces had gained

1

superiority in all these spheres and begun to threaten Spain's overseas interests [**doc. 1**] (**111** ch. 1). As early as 1618 Madrid had decided to renew the war with the Dutch when the truce came to an end (**163**), and in the three years before 1621 Spanish agents and troops were active in securing Spain's land-lines of communication from the Ligurian coast to the Netherlands.

This military life-line has been called the 'Spanish Road' (**57** ch. 3). It consisted of a string of fixed points – important bridges, ferries and fords – and the tracks between them. In fact the Road was a series of different 'roads' with semi-parallel itineraries which allowed Spanish troops to march northwards from Genoa into Lombardy and then across Savoy into Franche-Comté. The Dukes of Lorraine allowed Spanish troops to pass through their territories, provided they avoided the French troops stationed at Metz, Toul and Verdun. From Lorraine the Spaniards could move easily into Luxemburg and then through Liège either to Brussels or, via Jülich–Cleves and Münster, to the soft underbelly of the United Provinces – through Overijssel and Gelderland. However the Road was open to French intervention at almost any point in Franche-Comté and Lorraine, and relied on favourable political, dynastic and religious circumstances in the Cologne area and in north Italy. It was thus vulnerable at many points and any local crisis along its length would be bound to involve Spain.

For many years France had feared the consequences of being encircled by the Habsburgs. On the French southern frontier Rousillon was controlled by Spain; in the south-east the Republic of Genoa was a Spanish satellite; the Duchy of Milan was also Spanish territory; and many states in western Germany allowed Spanish troops to march along France's eastern border. As Spain sought to control her land-lines of communication more effectively after 1618, so France increased her efforts to hinder the process.

As early as 1601 Henry IV of France had forced Savoy (by the treaty of Lyon) to cede the district west of the river Rhone in order to threaten Spain's position in Milan. Henry also forced the Duke of Bouillon to allow the French to install a garrison in the stronghold of Sedan on the river Meuse and, in 1609, resisted Habsburg attempts to acquire Jülich–Cleves–Mark and Berg. Henry was on the point of going to war with Spain in 1610 when he was assassinated. The Regency of Marie de Medici and successive French governments up to 1624 avoided open conflict, but it was clear to Madrid that Spanish possessions in northern Italy, the

Upper Rhine and the Low Countries, were open targets for a strong and more belligerent French ruler.

In fact Spain considered that her most vulnerable possessions lay in northern Italy. The three most important states of northern and central Italy – Venice, the Duchy of Savoy–Piedmont, and the Papal States – were never considered by Madrid to be dependable. The Popes often doubted the wisdom of allowing the Papacy to become so dependent on Spain, and some of them attempted to build up France as a counter-weight. Clement VIII (1592–1605), for instance, restored Henry IV of France to the Catholic fold in 1595, brought Spain and France together to sign the peace of Vervins in 1598, and helped to form a strong French party in the College of Cardinals. Urban VIII (1623–44) sought to break the influence of both branches of the Habsburg family in Papal affairs.

Like some of the Popes, Venice also opposed the idea of a Habsburg hegemony in northern Italy. She was hemmed in by Austrian provinces to the east and north, the Spanish Duchy of Milan in the west and Spanish sympathisers in Mantua and Ferrara to the south. As with France, Venice constantly sought to prevent herself being encircled by the Habsburgs which often meant curbing Spanish influence in Italy.

The real maverick of the Italian political scene was Duke Charles Emmanuel of Savoy–Piedmont (**178**). He was to be a constant thorn in Spain's side and could never be trusted by Madrid. This was particularly worrying since the main lines of communication for Spain passed through Charles' lands. An alternative route to by-pass the Duchy of Savoy was one of Spain's top priorities. In 1593 Spain opened up a route through the Adda valley – known as the Valtelline – which led from the northern frontier of the Duchy of Milan through the Alps towards the Tyrol. This valley was part of the commonwealth of the Grisons – an area corresponding to the present-day canton of Graubünden. The Grisons were Protestants and in association with the Swiss Confederation. However the inhabitants of the Valtelline were Roman Catholic and Italian, and there was a long history of conflict with the Grisons, a conflict which had been exacerbated by international intrigue and family feuds.

France had already been involved in these local issues when she sought to use the route to get to Venice. Local family intrigues between the Plantas (Spanish supporters) and the Salis (French supporters) complicated the situation. The Grisons had given

France and Venice access to the Valtelline in 1602, but the Governor of Milan, fearing a French attack through the valley, built a fortress near Lake Como to make the Grisons change their minds. Charles Emmanuel of Savoy, during one of his anti-Spanish periods, expelled the Spanish garrisons in 1609 and, by the treaty of Brussolo (1610), agreed to invade Lombardy with the French. Only Henry IV's assassination prevented the offensive from taking place. However, this did not end the tension. The Alpine valleys now became a 'volcano of political, linguistic and religious instability ... The area was one of the cross–roads of European politics, where the messengers, troops and treasure of the Habsburg–Catholic axis going one way met those of the anti-Habsburg–Protestant axis going the other' (**29** p. 193).

In 1612, the Duke of Mantua, who controlled the fortresses of Montferrat and Casale, died without an immediate heir. In order to prevent Spain from gaining control, Charles Emmanuel made himself the master of Montferrat. However, the Governor of Milan, in retaliation, invaded Savoy, forcing Charles to withdraw from the fortress. Charles submitted his claim to Montferrat to imperial arbitration, but Spain was determined to prevent him from gaining control over it. After two military defeats Charles was forced to accept the treaty of Pavia which led, in 1620, to the re-opening of the Spanish Road. Yet it was clear to Madrid that the situation in Savoy was so volatile that no treaty would secure Spanish interests there for long.

When the Spanish–Dutch conflict re-started in 1621, the Dutch, lacking sufficient troops, were forced to enlist foreign mercenaries or subsidise foreign princes and their soldiers in an effort to extend the war and thereby keep the bulk of Spain's forces away from the Dutch frontier. In this manner the Dutch republicans came to support the Elector John Sigismund of Brandenburg in his struggle for Jülich–Cleves; they supported the rebellious nobles in Bohemia in their struggle against Habsburg absolutism and then, when the rebellion turned into a war, the Dutch encouraged those generals who were prepared to continue the fight for the Bohemian cause. The United Provinces became the focal-point of almost every anti–Habsburg coalition, involving first Denmark (1625) and then Sweden (1630) and France (1635). Spain attempted to prevent the widening of the conflict so that her resources could be concentrated more effectively against the Dutch. However, her attempts to do so drew her more and more into the problems of central and northern Europe.

Northern Europe

In northern Europe the repeated attempts of Denmark after 1523 to bring Sweden back into the Kingdom of Denmark–Norway failed, and the Danes lost many outposts in the eastern Baltic. This was fortunate for Sweden because a dynastic quarrel nearly wrecked her chances of remaining an independent Baltic power.

The Vasa King of Sweden, John III, managed to get his son, Sigismund, elected as his successor to the Polish throne (1587), and when John III died in 1592, Sigismund acquired the Swedish throne too. Yet Sigismund's rule proved unpopular and John III's brother, Duke Charles, with the support of the Swedish nobility, forced Sigismund to return to Poland in 1598. Charles now became the effective ruler of Sweden, and, in 1604, he formally assumed the Swedish throne as Charles (Karl) IX.

Fortunately for Charles, Sigismund III was faced with the Rokosz rebellion in Poland (1606–09), which prevented him from trying to reclaim his Swedish inheritance. However, Charles IX had to face increasing pressure from Denmark. Denmark–Norway still owned territory in central Sweden, and the Danish King, Christian IV, annoyed at recent Swedish expansion into the Arctic regions over which Denmark claimed sovereignty, eventually persuaded his nobles to attack Sweden in 1611. Charles IX died before the war ended, and his son, the seventeen-year-old Gustavus Adolphus, succeeded him, with the unenviable task of strengthening the power of a Vasa dynasty in Sweden that was on the verge of collapse.

However, with the help of the able Chancellor Axel Oxenstierna (1583–1654), Gustavus managed to bring the Danish war to a close with the peace of Knäred (1613). Although the Danes forced some concessions from the Swedes, including a huge indemnity for the return of Alvsborg – Sweden's only port on the North Sea – these proved only transitory and Sweden retained the right to trade through the Sound.

In the meantime, the quarrel between the Swedish and Polish branches of the Vasa family had led Sweden to seek closer ties with Russia. In 1609 Charles IX had agreed to offer the Tsar, Boris Gudunov, military assistance against Poland, in return for which Russia abandoned her claims to Livonia. Unfortunately, Poland also claimed Livonia and, partly to secure that claim, as well as to extend the power of the Vasa dynasty, Sigismund III attempted to make his son, the future Wladislaw IV of Poland, Tsar of Russia.

Although he succeeded in 1610, Wladislaw's rule was unpopular and ended in a general uprising against him. Michael Romanov took control in 1613 and asked for Swedish help to prevent a Polish invasion. Gustavus, wary of provoking a violent Polish reaction, allied with the Dutch (1614) and the Evangelical Union in Germany (1615) and forced Poland and Russia to make the agreement of Duelmo (1618) which eased Polish–Russian relations. Sweden's struggle with Poland was temporarily concluded with the truce of Tolsburg (1618), by which time Sweden was a power to be reckoned with in northern Europe.

Even so, the problems of the Baltic area had not been fully settled. Poland became the 'Spain of the North' and acted as a watch-dog for Madrid when the Dutch–Spanish conflict resumed in 1621. This development only served to heighten tension in the Baltic and directed the attention of both Denmark and Sweden to the affairs of northern Germany as they sought to guarantee the security of their possessions.

Thus for Spain and France, as also for the United Provinces, Sweden, Denmark and Poland, the affairs of central Europe came to have a growing influence on their separate local crises. All that was needed to transform these conflicts into a general European conflagration was a major crisis in the Holy Roman Empire.

The Holy Roman Empire

In theory, the Holy Roman Empire was the greatest state in western Europe. However, by the seventeenth century it was a mere shadow of the original 'Imperium Christianum' which had taken shape under Charlemagne on Christmas Day 800. Emperors and Popes had made uneasy allies, and the problem of supremacy had often asserted itself, culminating in the Investiture Contest of the eleventh century and the ultimate defeat of the Emperors. Charlemagne's Empire effectively ended with the death of Emperor Frederick II in 1250, though the title survived. From 1356 the holder of the Imperial title was Emperor of the 'Holy Roman Empire of the German Nation', which indicated more the weaknesses than the strengths of his authority. Originally elected 'Kings of Germany' and crowned Emperors at Rome by the Pope, from 1508 the Emperors insisted that their election itself conferred the Imperial title, and in any case that title had by this time become virtually hereditary in the Habsburg family.

The Empire covered a large area of central Europe, from the

Alps in the south to the Baltic in the north, and from France in the west to Poland and Hungary in the east (**Map 1**, pp. viii–ix). Yet at the beginning of the seventeenth century 'Germany' was less a political entity than a confused mass of princes and states, often referred to by contemporaries as 'the Germanies'. Although the Emperor was nominal ruler, real power lay with some fifty ecclesiastical and thirty secular Princes. Of these, the most important were the seven Electors who constituted the first Estate of the Imperial Diet (*Reichstag*) and who had the sole right to elect the Emperor: the Duke of Saxony, the Margrave of Brandenburg, the King of Bohemia, the Count Palatine of the Rhine, and the Archbishops of Mainz, Trier and Cologne.

The second Estate in the Diet was composed of the non-electoral Princes and the third Estate of some eighty Imperial Free Cities. Many of the smaller rulers, like the Counts, Prelates and 'Imperial Knights', guarded their privileges jealously and although a number of these formed confederations, there were still some three hundred distinct units within Germany. To an outsider, such a bewildering complexity was incomprehensible. Yet the variety of legal relationships was not totally senseless for those who relied on them (**77**). The Holy Roman Empire was much more an articulated system of checks and balances than appears at first sight, 'a living organism where appeal to the highest authority was always possible' (**19** p. 10).

In theory, the Princes were not absolute within their own domains, being limited by their allegiance to the Emperor and by the existence of representative assemblies of Estates consisting of nobles and towns (though rarely the peasants). Even so, in practice an able Prince could often get his own way. The Emperor himself had the added limitation of being part territorial magnate in his own right. From 1282 the Habsburgs had developed their family possessions based on the Danubian *Ostereich* and by the seventeenth century this patchwork of different territories – the inherited lands or *Erblande* – included Lower Austria (based on Vienna), Upper Austria (Linz), Inner Austria or Styria (Graz), Further Austria or *Vorlande* as well as Carinthia, Carniola, Istria, Trieste, Fiume, and the Tyrol. There were Habsburg territories beyond the bounds of the *Erblande*. Sections of Hungary were controlled by the Emperor and the lands of the crown of St Wenceslas – Bohemia, Moravia, Silesia, and Lusatia – came under Habsburg control in 1526 to create the Habsburg monarchy. There was general agreement in Austria that Bohemia was the major area within the crown lands, and when Rudolf II became Emperor in 1576, he made Prague his base.

However, the Emperors were not really strong even in their own territories. Ferdinand I had helped to create uncertainty by dividing the patrimony between his sons Maximilian II, who kept the Imperial title and the crowns of Hungary and Bohemia; Ferdinand, who gained the Tyrol; and Charles, who came to control Inner Austria or Styria. When Charles died in 1590, he was succeeded as ruler of Styria by his eldest son Ferdinand II, while his younger son, Leopold, eventually inherited the Tyrol. Maximilian's title and territories passed undivided to his eldest son Rudolf II in October 1576.

Rudolf II was a remarkable man (**19**), but his lack of assertiveness and his bouts of insanity allowed the government and administration of the Empire to be undermined. Gradually, much of the government of Austria and Hungary came to be taken over by Rudolf's third brother, Matthias. Yet the Emperor refused to delegate authority to Matthias, even though the latter was likely to be the next Emperor, and by the beginning of the seventeenth century relations between the main courts of the Habsburg lands were strained to breaking point.

It was fortunate for the Habsburgs that the Princes in the Empire were not united in opposition. The Elector of the Palatinate was the first secular Prince in Germany, outside the Imperial family. His territories were in two parts – the Rhenish or Lower Palatinate (a rich wine–growing district between the rivers Mosel, Saar and Rhine), and the Upper Palatinate (a relatively poor agricultural area between the Danube and Bohemia). By the seventeenth century the Elector, Frederick V, was a Calvinist. He was ably supported by his Chancellor, Christian of Anhalt, and they both sought to thwart the spread of the Catholic reformation. However, neither of these men was capable of gaining the trust of other German Princes or even of their nominal allies (**41** p. 35). Yet Frederick was always keen to attract outside support, especially from the United Provinces, but also from England, Bohemia, Austria and Hungary and the anti-Habsburg Catholic powers of Savoy, Venice and France. Thus any local crisis in this strategically important area in Europe was bound to attract international concern.

The Elector of Saxony, John George, was thirty years old in 1618. He was conservative and Lutheran. Often drunk and, to the diplomats who dealt with him, uncultured, John George's position was never clear or well-stated. He had no mission apart from the maintenance of peace, commercial prosperity and the preservation of the ancient 'German Liberties' in the face of Habsburg absolutism. John George sought to defend Lutheranism against its Calvinist and Catholic enemies. Yet there were to be times when people felt betrayed by John Geroge: the Protestants in 1620, the Emperor in 1631 and the Swedes in 1635. Nobody really knew which side John George supported, and although he was honest in his desire for peace, there was always doubt about the nature of the peace that would satisfy him.

Maximilian of Bavaria, a small man with a shrill voice, was thought by many observers to be one of the ablest of German Princes. By 1618 he was forty-five and had ruled Bavaria for twenty years. His passion for administration enabled Bavaria to boast a stable and solvent government, but he interfered in the private concerns of his subjects and ruthlessly punished adulterers and witches. He was mean to his subjects and mean to Germany. He never committed himself to any political initiative for any great length of time and his championship of the Habsburg–Catholic cause in 1609 was soon to be reversed as he sought to exclude the Habsburgs from the Catholic League – which he designed to serve his own purposes. He even suggested that his League and the Evangelical Union might unite to preserve 'German Liberties' from Spanish–Austrian encroachments. Because of this, he seemed to the Emperor Ferdinand II to be an opponent and rival.

The Elector of Brandenburg, John Sigismund, had the largest territories but the poorest possessions in the north-eastern plain of Germany. In 1618 he inherited Prussia and thus gained – in Königsberg – an outlet to the sea. Most of his subjects were Lutheran, but John Sigismund was a Calvinist. However, he did little to annoy the Habsburgs for fear of Polish intervention in his newly acquired fief. Old and harassed by court intrigues, John Sigismund was more concerned to follow the lead of John George of Saxony. Yet the very fragmented nature of this Hohenzollern collection of territories was to force the future Electors into improving internal communications and centralising their power.

Thus, divisions amongst the Princes and between the leading members of the Austrian Habsburgs created an unstable situation in central Europe. This instability worried those outside powers, like Spain, who depended on a strong Habsburg presence in that region. There were a number of general problems within the Empire which periodically produced local crises and which required prompt and firm action if the Habsburg family hoped to retain its hold on the Imperial title. Increasingly Spain was drawn into them in order to support her ailing Austrian relations, but such a development posed a threat to the general peace of Europe.

Many of these problems stemmed from religious developments in the sixteenth century. After the Reformation the majority of German Princes were Protestant, though they were far from being united. This was especially so after the Augsburg 'Interim' of 1547 and the religious peace of Augsburg of 1555. By the former, some concessions were made by the Emperor to Protestants – such as clerical marriage and communion in both kinds – but in return they were to conform to Catholic doctrine. Obviously, many Protestant Princes and their subjects did not co-operate, even though Philip Melanchthon, Luther's spiritual heir, conditionally accepted the Interim. Protestantism was divided. Followers of Melanchthon – the 'Philippists' – wanted to accept some of the ideas of Calvin and Zwingli concerning the eucharist and predestination, but they were opposed by the hard-line Lutherans who, after Melanchthon's death in 1577, produced the 'Formula of Concord' to define their position clearly. As a consequence, the Philippists drew closer to the Calvinists, and some important areas of Germany – such as the Palatinate, Bremen, Anhalt, and Hesse – accepted Calvinism as their faith.

This development was doubly unfortunate for the unity and survival of Protestantism in central Europe. The Lutheran–Calvinist doctrinal split prevented the formation of a common front against attempts by the Catholic church to regain its lost supporters and territory. The peace of Augsburg in 1555 exacerbated the Protestant split. It officially recognised the existence of Lutherans but not Zwinglians, Calvinists or Anabaptists, leaving the ruler of each state free to decide which of the two main faiths he would accept for his dominions. Those subjects who would not accept a ruler's decision were allowed to sell their property and leave. The Free Cities were to treat Protestants and Catholics equally.

The ecclesiastical principalities presented a real problem for the Emperor. There was the danger that the Prince–Bishops who ruled these territories might adopt Protestantism and establish their new régimes on confiscated Catholic property. Even more dangerous was the possibility that one or more of the three electoral bishoprics of Mainz, Cologne and Trier might fall into Protestant hands. With this in mind, the Emperor drew up an 'Ecclesiastical Reservation', according to which any ecclesiastical ruler who changed his faith was to forfeit his office, and a Catholic was to be elected in his place. This was opposed by the Protestant Princes and it was not actually included in the formal peace terms of 1555. However, the Emperor forced the issue by making the formal peace hinge on a general acceptance of a supplementary Imperial Edict which embodied the 'Reservation'. The Princes accepted it only with reluctance. They had won important rights, embodied in the legal maxim *cuius regio, eius religio* – 'the ruler of a territory shall determine its religion'. This formula led to a hardening of religious feeling within the Empire.

There were a number of Catholic successes in the ensuing years. In the 1580s, the Archbishop–Elector of Cologne had wanted to convert to Lutheranism in order to secularise his principality. He was immediately deposed by the Emperor who called in Spanish troops to ensure the maintenance of Catholic interests under a Catholic replacement. In 1608, the Duke of Bavaria, in the name of the Emperor, put down a Protestant rising in the Imperial City of Donauworth near Augsburg. The Protestant Estates, assembled at the Imperial Diet in Regensburg, objected to this action, claiming that it breached the 1555 agreements. The Catholics demanded that all ecclesiastical property that had been secularised since that date – such as the bishoprics of Magdeburg and Halberstadt – should be restored. Most of the Protestant Estates, led by the Palatinate and Brandenburg, spurned these demands and established a defensive alliance – the Protestant (or Evangelical) Union. It included nine Princes and seventeen Imperial Cities under the leadership of the Elector Palatine. Its 'general' was Christian of Anhalt, and its main outside supporter was Henry IV of France (**170**).

Many observers saw this as a dangerous move towards anarchy, not only in the Empire but in the Protestant movement generally. The Union was mostly Calvinist in character and many Lutherans, including the Elector of Saxony, held aloof, mistrusting the strain of resistance that Calvinism introduced to the political affairs of central Europe.

Maximilian I of Bavaria reacted to this Protestant challenge by forming the Catholic League in 1609. The Austrian Habsburgs were not asked to join it, revealing how far the Emperor's authority had declined in his dealings with the Princes. Significantly, Philip III of Spain felt compelled to send the League financial support for fear that lack of Austrian involvement would damage Habsburg prestige and influence still further at a time when a renewal of religious war in central Europe seemed imminent. Just how important it was for Spain to have a strong Emperor in Vienna or Prague was revealed by the crisis over the strategically important principality of Jülich–Cleves.

The duchies of Jülich, Cleves, Mark, Berg and Ravensberg stretched along the Rhine and although ruled by one family were a mixture of religious persuasions. Jülich and Berg had remained Catholic; Mark and Ravensberg had converted to Lutheranism; while Cleves had become Calvinist. In 1609, the Duke of Jülich–Cleves died without a male heir. Rudolf II appointed his nephew, Leopold, as Imperial Commissary to take possession of the duchies pending a full legal inquiry. However, the descendants of the late Duke's sisters – John Sigismund, Elector of Brandenburg, and Wolfgang William, son of the Count Palatine of Neuburg – both claimed the duchies, and when Leopold seized Jülich in Rudolf's name the two Princes agreed on a joint occupancy – the treaty of Dortmund, 1609.

The French and Dutch were soon drawn in to support the Protestant claimants and Maurice of Orange led a force to capture Jülich and install a Dutch garrison. With France ready to intervene, an international conflict seemed inevitable. However, Henry IV of France was assassinated before he could launch a full-scale campaign and the death of the Emperor Rudolf II in 1612 led to a search for compromise. Wolfgang William converted to Roman Catholicism and married the sister of Maximilian of Bavaria in the hope that this might bring him the support of the Catholic League and eventually possession of all the duchies. John Sigismund adopted Calvinism with a similar end in view, but with the support of the Palatinate, the Netherlands and England. Fortunately for the general peace of Europe, the major outside interests were not in a position to wage all-out war over the issue and they brought the two Princes to compromise by the treaty of Xanten (November 1614). Brandenburg retained control of the predominantly Protestant duchies of Cleves, Mark and Ravensberg, while Neuburg gained possession of the mainly Catholic Jülich and Berg.

However, it was clear that the religious divisions were hardening in central Europe, and that they were attracting foreign military and financial support. The new Emperor, Matthias, seemed powerless to prevent the situation degenerating further. His chief adviser, Cardinal Khlesl, sought to soften the attitudes of the hard-liners in both camps. He managed to get Austria admitted to the Catholic League in 1613, which led Maximilian of Bavaria to withdraw his support and it was dissolved in 1617. Khlesl was not alone in seeking conciliation, and he was supported by the Archbishop of Mainz and the Lutheran Elector of Saxony. Indeed, the Protestant Union was divided after the withdrawal of Neuburg in 1614, followed by Brandenburg in 1617, and its nominal head – the Elector Palatine – was never able to rely on its support. Even so, the prospects for peace in Europe were not good and a crisis in Bohemia set in train a course of events which produced a European conflagration.

The Bohemian crisis

From the time of the Hussite wars of the 1420s, Bohemia's Catholics, Calvinists, Lutherans, Utraquists and Anabaptists ('Bohemian Brethren') had coexisted in relative harmony. When Rudolf II set up his court in Prague, about two-thirds of the population of Bohemia was Protestant and a mere one-tenth Roman Catholic – though the proportion of nobility who were Catholic was much higher. Although Rudolf would have liked to expel Protestantism from his domains, he was aware that it would require a major upheaval to accomplish the task, and in any case he sought the support of the Bohemian Estates against his ambitious brother Matthias. In the 'Letter of Majesty' of July 1609, the Estates exacted a high price for this support: freedom of conscience for all Bohemian subjects; liberty of worship for the nobles and those towns which belonged to the crown; and control of ecclesiastical organisation within the kingdom to rest with the Estates [**doc. 3**].

Rudolf never viewed these arrangements as being permanent, and in 1611, with the help of his nephew, the Archduke Leopold, he attempted a *coup d'état* to restore his authority in Bohemia. The Bohemian Estates appealed to Matthias, who willingly came to their assistance and thwarted Rudolf's plan. In return, the Estates elected Matthias as their King and for the next five years there was relative peace. Matthias became Emperor in 1612 but remained childless, and the other leading Austrian Habsburgs decided that he should be succeeded as Emperor by the Archduke Ferdinand of Styria, a hard-line Catholic. In 1617 they proposed that, as a first step towards this end, Ferdinand should be made King of Bohemia and Hungary.

However, the Bohemian Estates were not prepared to accept a new King without an election and the Protestants were opposed to Ferdinand on the grounds that he would attempt to impose Habsburg absolutism at their expense. Yet the Protestants were divided over a suitable alternative candidate – the Lutherans favoured the Elector of Saxony and the Calvinists wanted the Elector Palatine. Eventually, in June 1617, after much confusion, the Estates formally accepted Ferdinand as King of Bohemia on the condition that he guaranteed the Letter of Majesty. Although Ferdinand initially consented to this demand, he never felt bound by the Letter, and he soon showed his intention to weaken the Protestants' position. Of the ten Deputies he appointed to rule Bohemia, only three were Protestant.

While Ferdinand was in Vienna making arrangements for the Imperial succession, the Deputies questioned whether two new Protestant churches at Klostergrab and Brunau were 'legal' in the sense of being on royal land and therefore protected by the Letter. The government asserted that the land was no longer royal, and a deputation sent from Klostergrab to contest the decision was arrested. A section of the nobility led by Count Thurn appealed to Ferdinand on the grounds that the Letter was being infringed.

The swiftness of the reply, which discounted their objections, led the nobility to suspect that their appeal had been blocked by the Catholic Deputies and they summoned a national assembly. When it met in May 1618, the nobles decided to confront the Deputies in person. The result was the famous 'Defenestration of Prague' when the two Catholic Deputies suspected of being at the heart of the anti-Protestant policies – Martinitz and Slavata – along with an unfortunate clerk, were thrown out of a window of the Hradschin palace. It was a symbolic act – the accepted manner of asserting Bohemian autonomy against a threatening occupying power – and it was meant to be seen as a deliberate challenge to the Emperor's use of 'Evil Councillors'. To that extent it mattered little that the victims survived their ordeal.

The Protestant nobles, with the approval of the Estates, appointed thirty-six 'Directors' to administer Bohemia. A national militia was planned, under Thurn's command, but there was not enough money and the recruits were poorly equipped and lacking in military skill. The Bohemian Directors called on the Estates of all the Habsburg lands to join them in defence of political 'Liberties' and religious toleration, but there was little initial response. Even some Bohemian towns opposed the activities of the Directors, and the peasants, exploited by those very 'Liberties' the nobles wanted to preserve, were not enthusiastic. There was little basis for a patriotic and religious crusade. Thus, the nobles had to confine their protests within the limits of the existing social order, and to be successful they clearly required the support of foreign powers.

The Dutch vaguely promised material assistance, but it was left to Charles Emmanuel of Savoy to send a mercenary commander, Ernst von Mansfeld, and 2,000 men – acting in the name of the Elector Palatine. This raised the Directors' hopes that the forces of the Evangelical Union would intervene to support Mansfeld. However, though Christian of Anhalt wanted to help, the Union was in no position to provide money or men for the Bohemian cause.

On 20 March 1619, Matthias died and it was clear that his successor would be Ferdinand. Since there was also little doubt that Ferdinand would press forward with a policy of re-Catholicisation – despite the moderation counselled by Cardinal Khlesl – Lusatia, Silesia and Moravia decided to support the rebel cause in Bohemia. Even the Estates in Upper Austria opposed Ferdinand. Bethlen Gabor, Prince of Transylvania, led a revolt in Hungary, and Thurn led an army towards Vienna – though he was forced to retreat before he could capture it.

In July 1619 Bohemia, Lusatia, Silesia and Moravia inaugurated a new constitution by an Act of Confederation. According to the Act, the Bohemian crown was to remain elective; Austria and Hungary were to be incorporated if the circumstances were right; the Letter of Majesty, and Protestant privileges, were to be guaranteed; and crown lands and confiscated Catholic properties were to pay for the defence of the Confederation. It was clear that a new King was needed.

The Lutherans looked to the Elector of Saxony, John George, but he was more concerned with his own position and he would not challenge Ferdinand's right to the Bohemian throne. This left the Calvinist Elector Palatine – Frederick V. His father-in-law was James I of England and this connection offered the rebels the hope that England would be prepared to fight to uphold the Protestant cause in Europe. However, James I was loath to support Frederick V and he would have agreed with the depressing prognostication of Count Solms, the Palatine ambassador at Frankfurt, that

If it is true ... the Bohemians are about to depose Ferdinand
and elect another King, let everyone prepare at once for war
lasting twenty, thirty, or forty years. The Spaniards and the
House of Austria will deploy all their worldly goods to recover
Bohemia; indeed the Spaniards would rather lose the
Netherlands than allow their House to lose control of Bohemia
so disgracefully and so outrageously (**29** p. 163).

15

Yet on 26 August 1619 the Bohemian Estates duly declared the throne to be vacant and offered the crown to Frederick V. Two days later, at Frankfurt-on-Main, Ferdinand was elected as Emperor. When Frederick – who had decided to accept the proffered crown – arrived in Prague in October 1619 the war-clouds were gathering fast, and the starkness of his position was alarming.

Spanish diplomatic activity increased sharply. Madrid encouraged Sigismund of Poland to prevent an intervention by Gustavus Adolphus and to keep a watching-brief on the movements of the unpredictable Bethlen Gabor in the east. A Spanish fleet was sent to Flanders and the important Rhine crossing at Breisach was strengthened. Plans were made for the occupation of the Lower Palatinate. Philip III of Spain thought that 'these measures are so urgent ... Germany simply cannot be lost' (**26** p. 64). The Spanish general in Flanders, Spinola, advised Philip that ultimate victory over the Dutch depended on the defeat of the Bohemian rebels for

> ... it is quite possible that the House of Austria may be turned out of Germany bag and baggage. If the Protestants succeed in doing this they will then join the Dutch in an attack upon these provinces, not only as a return for the help which they are getting from them, but because they will imagine that whilst your Majesty's forces are here, they will not be left undisturbed in the enjoyment of their new possessions. If all the German and Dutch Protestants were to unite in attacking us after a victory in Germany it would be hopeless for us to attempt to resist them (**26** p. 68).

In July 1620, Spinola moved his forces from Flanders into the Palatinate and took over Frederick's possessions on the left bank of the Rhine. Maximilian of Bavaria, although he had re-formed the Catholic League in 1617 without asking the Emperor to join it, now offered to put the League's forces at Ferdinand's disposal. His motives were not really altruistic. He feared Spanish plans to intervene in the Palatinate, since the Emperor had secretly promised him that the electoral title would be transferred to Bavaria. Ferdinand accepted his offer, and in July 1620 Maximilian's army – some 30,000 strong under the command of Count von Tilly – moved into Austria and forced the Austrian Estates to break their alliance with the Bohemian rebels. From there Tilly marched into Bohemia.

John George of Saxony sent his men into Lusatia, not as part of a counter-move, but to protect the territory Ferdinand had promised him if he remained aloof from the rebel cause. Frederick's army, under Christian of Anhalt and Thurn, faced the enemy alone. Previous appeals for help to England and the Dutch had not been successful. The Dutch offered only 5,000 troops and a subsidy of 50,000 florins a month. James I had opposed Frederick's decision to accept the Bohemian throne and, with Anglo–Dutch relations soured by a dispute over fishing grounds, felt ill-disposed towards any joint action. The French had managed to persuade the frightened members of the Evangelical Union and the Catholic League to recognise each other's neutrality in the treaty of Ulm in 1620 – though this left Maximilian the right to fight Bohemia. On 8 November 1620 the Imperial army routed Christian of Anhalt in just over an hour on the White Mountain, to the west of Prague. Frederick V, the 'Winter King', was forced into exile and the Bohemians were left to their fate.

Even before the White Mountain, Ferdinand had begun to transfer rebel possessions to his commanders, partly to reward them and partly to keep their armies together. Regional Commissions were established in November 1620 to define the Emperor's rights over property belonging to the rebels. In June 1621 twenty-seven rebels were executed, and by the end of the year 486 estates had been confiscated. All Protestant ministers were compelled to leave Bohemia in 1624, and in 1627 all Bohemian subjects were forced to make the choice between exile or Catholicism. When an Imperial decree enforced this re-Catholicisation, some 30,000 families emigrated. Between 1615 and 1650 Bohemia's population fell by 50 per cent. By a Patent of 1624 the obligations of the peasantry to their masters were increased, which prompted a full-scale peasant rebellion in Bohemia and Moravia, and, in May 1626, there was a dangerous peasant rebellion in Upper Austria.

However, the Habsburgs continued to impose their absolutist policies. By a 'renewed constitution' of 10 May 1627, Bohemia was declared a hereditary possession of the Habsburgs. This constitution also abolished the rights of towns and the nobility, and reinforced the powers of the Commissioners. German became the official language, and the Catholic faith became the only permissible religion. The battle of the White Mountain had sealed the fate of Protestantism in Bohemia and left Catholic, including Spanish, forces in control of strategically important areas in central Europe. This was a state of affairs the remaining Protestant Princes in Germany and other European powers could not tolerate for long.

Part Two: Developments, 1621–48

2 The Habsburgs in the Ascendant

In January 1621 Ferdinand placed Frederick V under an Imperial ban and then ordered Maximilian of Bavaria to occupy the Palatinate. The German Princes and cities of the Protestant Union met at Heilbronn and protested at the Emperor's arbitrary actions. Yet in April Ferdinand managed to get the Princes to agree to the Mainz Accord which called for the disbanding of Union forces. On 24 May the Union was dissolved, never to meet again.

Significantly, the more bellicose of the Princes of the Union – such as the Margrave of Baden, Count von Mansfeld, and Duke Christian of Brunswick – refused to sign the Accord and kept their forces in the field. Christian IV of Denmark, along with the United Provinces, was very concerned at the presence of Spanish troops in part of the Lower Palatinate and at the turn of events in central Europe. The Dutch allowed the exiled Frederick V to set up his court at the Hague and solicited the military support of the Duke of Brunswick and Mansfeld.

However, these commanders mostly led mercenary armies which lived off the land and proved a constant source of anxiety to local landholders and peasantry. Very rarely did they have a coherent strategy, but throughout the years 1622–26 they succeeded in recruiting sufficient troops to fight a series of *ad hoc* campaigns which kept central Europe in turmoil.

At first they were successful. Tilly, in command of the Catholic League forces, was defeated at Wiesloch in April 1622. However, he soon had his revenge at Wimpfen and Höchst. Frederick V had joined the united forces of Mansfeld and Brunswick in April 1622 but these defeats forced him to return to the Hague. His intervention had been a serious miscalculation. Until then, many people in Germany, and even the King of Spain, had felt that the Imperial ban had been too harsh and ought to be lifted. After the events of 1622, however, Frederick was seen as a rebel and this gave Ferdinand the opportunity to gain support for his policies at a general electoral meeting at Regensburg in 1623.

At this meeting, Ferdinand proposed that Frederick V should be deprived of his electoral dignity and his lands and that both should be transferred to Maximilian of Bavaria. To overcome the reservations of Saxony and Brandenburg – whose rulers had deliberately absented themselves from the meeting – Ferdinand offered Lusatia to John George and rights over East Prussia to George William of Brandenburg. The suspicious Catholic Princes were assured that the transfer would give Catholic Electors a majority of five to two and thus save the Catholic cause in Germany. Ferdinand's proposals were put into effect in February 1623.

It might be supposed that James I of England could have done more to help his son-in-law in his hour of need. The Dutch had tried to persuade the English to intervene in the Palatinate after the battle of the White Mountain, but it was clear that the English Parliament was not prepared to finance a military expedition. At the same time, the projected Spanish match between James I's son, Prince Charles, and the Spanish Infanta, kept the English King lukewarm towards a policy of military intervention in Europe.

Even so, Frederick's return to the Hague in 1622 did not prevent Mansfeld and Christian of Brunswick from marching to attack Bavaria. Maximilian used Tilly to head off the threat, and before the mercenary leaders could join forces, Brunswick was heavily defeated at Stadtlohn in August 1623. Mansfeld did not have sufficient resources to operate alone, and in 1624 he travelled to London to seek financial support.

This time his pleas did not fall on deaf ears. The Spanish marriage project had ended in humiliation in Madrid after Prince Charles and the Duke of Buckingham had gone to Spain in an attempt to quicken proceedings. Thus James I's attitude towards Spain had hardened and Mansfeld was given permission to raise 12,000 men in England for use in a Palatine campaign.

The Grisons issue and the Valtelline

Until 1622 the French government had been preoccupied with internal problems, but after the treaty of Montpellier in that year it felt free to pressurise the Spaniards in Italy. In 1623 the French made an alliance with Venice and Savoy to eject Spanish troops from the Valtelline (the treaty of Paris). Conditions in the passes seemed ripe for exploitation. Since 1613 and the ending of the Grison alliance with Venice, the Habsburgs had tried to bind the Grisons to the Empire in order to keep the Spanish Road open. However, economic adversity had given radicals like George

Jenatsch a popular appeal in the Valtelline and a period of anti-Catholic activities (1618–19) had resulted in a hardening of religious divisions in the area. The treaty of Madrid between France and Spain in April 1621 preserved some rights for Protestants in the valleys but provided for Spain's continued use of the route. The Catholics in the Valtelline objected to the idea of religious toleration and in January 1622, with Habsburg support, they imposed the Articles of Milan which abolished the Grison Confederation and left the Habsburgs free to use the passes.

At this point, with the treaty of Paris threatening to bring France, Venice and Savoy into a war with Spain and the Imperial forces in Italy, Olivares asked for the Pope's protection for the Catholic inhabitants of the Valtelline. The Pope responded by sending Papal troops to occupy Spanish fortresses. This put a temporary halt to French plans to implement the provisions of the treaty of Paris.

However, in 1624 Richelieu attained power in France and aimed to restore France's name abroad. Early in 1625, French troops, with Swiss support, drove out the Papal garrisons and closed the Valtelline. Yet the *Dévots* party in France objected to the use of French troops against Papal forces and this created such a delicate domestic political situation that when Spanish troops from Milan reoccupied the Valtelline, Richelieu felt too vulnerable to risk an open war. He reluctantly accepted the treaty of Monzon in March 1626, which left Spain with the use of the Alpine valley. Even so it was clear to Spain that, with Richelieu shaping French foreign policy, such periods of relative calm in northern Italy and along the Spanish Road would be of short duration.

The formation of the Hague Coalition

There was growing opposition to Spanish policies in other areas of Europe. Maximilian of Bavaria remained suspicious of Spain's presence in part of the Palatinate and his intransigence prevented Spinola from making a massive assault on the United Provinces when the Twelve Years Truce ended in 1621. This gave the Dutch the opportunity to negotiate the treaty of Compiègne with England and France in 1624 which reflected the hardening of attitudes towards Spain in many European countries. However, Maximilian now took alarm and, in desperation, pledged his support for the Emperor (**156**).

A major Spanish offensive against the Dutch was then possible and it began fully in the campaign season of 1625. Olivares wanted a joint military and commercial venture with the aim of disrupting Dutch trade with the Baltic. In June 1625, Spinola captured Breda, thereby capitalising on the blow the Dutch had suffered with the death of Prince Maurice in April. Prince Frederick Henry, Maurice's successor, had yet to prove himself and the Dutch desperately sought outside help. Gustavus Adolphus of Sweden offered them his military assistance to help restore Silesia, Bohemia and Moravia to Frederick V. However, the Dutch mistrusted the Swedish King's intentions and in any case England preferred an alliance with King Christian IV of Denmark, who also offered his services. The Coalition of the Hague which was finalised in December 1625 thus included England, the United Provinces, Denmark and the Lower Saxon Circle. It had the sympathy of Bethlen Gabor, the Turkish *Porte* and Frederick V. The Bohemian exiles at the Hague hoped that the Coalition would eventually enable them to return home, though ominously for them no mention of the Bohemian issue was made in the negotiations.

The Danish war, 1626–29

The Coalition planned a three-pronged attack on the Habsburgs. Christian IV was to march into north-west Germany, Christian of Brunswick hoped to enter the Rhineland, and Mansfeld was to join forces with Bethlen Gabor in the vicinity of Bohemia. However, Christian IV, as a German Prince in his own right, was more interested in controlling Lower Saxony along with the Protestant bishoprics of Bremen, Verden, Minden and Halberstadt, as well as the Hansa cities of Hamburg and Lubeck, than he was in pressing forward into Bohemia. With control of Bremen and Verden he intended to monitor trade along the rivers Weser and Elbe and enhance Denmark's monopoly of Baltic commerce. In May 1625 Christian IV persuaded the states of the Lower Saxon Circle to elect him as their president so that he could justify the use of his army to defend their 'Liberties'. Yet the Dutch, English and French could only offer him moral support and Christian found it very difficult to co-ordinate military policy with the other Coalition commanders. More significantly, Ferdinand II had begun to strengthen his own military position.

In late 1624 the Emperor had authorised one of his Czech subjects – Albrecht von Waldenstein, or Wallenstein – to raise an army which would reduce Ferdinand's dependence on the Catholic

League forces under Tilly. Marriage to a wealthy widow had given Wallenstein the opportunity to speculate in property confiscated from the Bohemian rebels, and by 1623 he had come to own about a quarter of Bohemia and been appointed military governor of Prague. In April 1625 Wallenstein was created *Generalissimo* of all Imperial troops and, after recruiting 24,000 men, was elevated to the rank of Duke of Friedland in June 1625 (**55**).

Wallenstein and Tilly proved a formidable military combination. Mansfeld was defeated by Wallenstein at Dessau bridge in April 1626 and was forced to retreat through Brandenburg into Silesia. Christian IV of Denmark was routed by Tilly at Lutter, near Brunswick, in August 1626 and by late 1627 the Danish King had been driven back into his own kingdom. Although Christian IV did not make peace until 1629, it was clear that the Protestant offensive had been repelled. If Mansfeld had hoped that by marching eastwards he might join with Bethlen Gabor, he was to be disappointed, for the Transylvanian Prince had come to terms with the Emperor. In November 1626, with his troops deserting him, and still without any clear policy, Mansfeld died at Sarajevo. Ferdinand was thus secure in the greater part of Germany.

Having put down a peasants' revolt in Austria in 1626, the Emperor completed the subjugation of Bohemia and supported Wallenstein's progress into Mecklenburg in 1628. Wallenstein was rewarded with the lands and ducal title of Mecklenburg and was appointed 'General of the whole Imperial Fleet and Lord of the Atlantic and Baltic'. Imperial forces thus gained control of the important ports of Wismar and Rostock, and this gave Olivares the opportunity to urge the adoption of his plan to unite the trading towns of Flanders and the Hansa and thereby wrest control of the carrying trade between the Baltic and southern Europe from the United Provinces. With Wismar in Imperial hands the way was open for the application of this *almirantazgo* policy (see ch. 5, pp. 56). Spain's economic fortunes needed a boost, since Olivares' government was bankrupt in 1627 and Castile was forced to demand that the other kingdoms of the Spanish monarchy should contribute more money. This project, the Union of Arms, aroused considerable opposition and Aragon, Catalonia, and Valencia refused aid. Olivares was forced to resort to borrowing once again and there were fears that Spain was seriously over-reaching herself. The *almirantazgo* policy appeared to be a remedy for Spain's financial ills, at the same time as it offered an opportunity for Spain to disrupt the Dutch economy.

However, Wallenstein was not a willing supporter of this policy at first. He had never understood the importance of naval superiority and in any case Lubeck and Danzig, two of the most important Hansa towns, refused to co-operate. Wallenstein intended to use Mecklenburg as a nucleus for his expanding personal empire and he was not keen to encourage an increase in Spanish influence in northern Germany.

Yet Denmark remained master of the seas and in his attempt to besiege Stralsund, in July 1628, Wallenstein was made painfully aware of the need for a strong Imperial navy. The town refused to capitulate and gained the assistance of Denmark and Sweden, who temporarily sank their differences to combat Habsburg imperialism. Without a navy, Wallenstein was forced to abandon the siege. The Dutch pressed home the lesson of naval superiority when, in 1628 at Matanzas bay near Cuba, Piet Heyn destroyed a third of the Spanish ships employed in the West India trade and captured 11 million florins in booty (see Note, p. vi).

The humiliation of Stralsund also made Wallenstein aware of the growing power of Sweden. He therefore began to seek a speedy end to the Danish war. After inflicting another crushing defeat on the Danes at Wolgast in September 1628, he persuaded Ferdinand II to offer Christian IV generous peace terms. By the treaty of Lubeck of June 1629, Denmark was allowed to keep her possessions – including Holstein – but was forced to abandon her claims on the north German bishoprics. Christian IV was also persuaded to give up his leadership of the Lower Saxon Circle.

The Edict of Restitution, 1629

With Denmark out of the war, Ferdinand thought he was in a strong enough position to restore the religious and territorial situation that had existed in the Empire after the peace of Augsburg in 1555. On 6 March 1629, without consulting the Princes or gaining the approval of the Imperial Diet, Ferdinand issued the Edict of Restitution [**Doc 4**], with the aim of imposing the controversial 'Ecclesiastical Reservation' of 1555. It affected the two secularised archbishoprics of Bremen and Magdeburg, twelve bishoprics and more than a hundred religious houses as well as some towns. Calvinists were again refused the benefits of the Augsburg Agreement. The result of the Edict was a great transfer of property and power from Protestants to Catholics which entailed the re-drawing of boundaries all over north and central Germany and the destruction of some property rights that had existed for three generations.

However, the possession and administration of dioceses, monasteries and religious foundations was as much a political and financial matter as a religious one, and the Protestants were not alone in being alarmed at the manner in which the Edict had been issued. More disturbing still was the intended use of Wallenstein and his army to deal with any armed resistance.

Wallenstein, who now had 134,000 men in the field, was as much a threat to the Princes of the Empire as he was to the Emperor's enemies, for it seemed that Ferdinand was determined to use the Edict of Restitution, backed by Wallenstein's army, to establish himself as absolute monarch with wide dictatorial powers. In fairness, Wallenstein disliked the Edict and did not enforce it as harshly as he might have done, but he had aroused the opposition of a growing band of influential nobles, led by Maximilian of Bavaria, and this group began to put pressure on the Emperor to dismiss him [**doc. 10**].

The Regensburg meeting of Electors, 1630

The Emperor summoned the Electors to meet at Regensburg in the summer of 1630. The Protestant Electors, John George of Saxony and George William of Brandenburg, refused to attend the meeting in protest at the Edict of Restitution. Maximilian of Bavaria and the Elector of Mainz attended, but only to raise the issue of 'German Liberties'. The Emperor wanted the agreement of the Electors on two proposals. The first was the election of his son as King of the Romans. The second was increased imperial involvement in the Dutch war and in north Italy. The Electors saw that Germany had little to gain from a war against the United Provinces and instead Maximilian of Bavaria, their leader, pressed for the dismissal of Wallenstein.

In the hope of softening the Electors' attitude, Ferdinand dismissed his *Generalissimo* on 24 August 1630. However, the Electors did not give way over the Emperor's two proposals and he in turn refused to withdraw the Edict of Restitution. Yet Ferdinand's position had weakened considerably, because of the landing of Gustavus Adolphus in Pomerania in the previous month with an expeditionary force of some 4,000 men. No one knew what Gustavus would do or where he would go, but his presence meant that Ferdinand II was once more dependent on the military assistance of Maximilian and Tilly.

The Mantuan war, 1627–31

The Regensburg meeting had also been a setback for France over
the Mantuan question. In December 1627, the last Gonzaga heir to
the duchy of Milan had died and Duke Charles of Nevers–Gonzaga
– the French claimant – took possession. Yet Mantua was legally
an imperial fief, and Ferdinand had already promised it to Spain.
Montferrat, also part of the ducal territories, was claimed by Spain
and Savoy who divided it up between themselves. Charles Emmanuel of Savoy had long desired to control the fortress of Casale in
Montferrat, since it dominated the strategically important route
from Milan to Genoa. Yet the fortress refused to accept Spanish–
Savoyard control and had to be besieged by the Spaniards.

France saw this as a good opportunity to humiliate Spain and
assert her own continuing interest in Italy, and in March 1629
Louis XIII crossed the Alps with his troops and relieved Casale.
France avoided a formal declaration of war, but gave Spain a clear
indication of her anti-Habsburg foreign policy. Yet as soon as
Louis XIII returned to France, Wallenstein's army marched
through the Valtelline and took possession of Mantua. This
allowed the Spaniards to renew their siege of Casale. Richelieu
retaliated in 1630 by occupying Savoy and capturing Pinerolo,
although he could not prevent Wallenstein strengthening his position in Mantua. However, the Spanish commander, Spinola, died
outside Casale and the fortress managed to hold out.

The French envoys at Regensburg had assumed that Casale
would fall and therefore negotiated a treaty with the Emperor
(treaty of Regensburg) which was unfavourable to France. By it
Ferdinand was to recognise Nevers as Duke of Mantua, but was to
receive Casale and Pinerolo. France also promised not to interfere
in the internal affairs of the Empire. Thus, France's bridgehead
into Italy and her involvement in Imperial affairs, both so important for Richelieu's aims in Europe, appeared lost.

Richelieu was furious with his ambassadors and, taking advantage of the increasing pressure on Ferdinand resulting from the
Regensburg meeting and the invasion by Sweden, he insisted on a
re-negotiation of the terms of the treaty, which was accomplished
by the peace of Cherasco of 1631. This time the Emperor agreed to
recognise Nevers as Duke of Mantua without any of the previous
commitments on the part of the French. All troops were to be
withdrawn from northern Italy, although France retained Pinerolo
and thus maintained a bridgehead if it should be needed.

3 Gustavus Adolphus, Wallenstein and the Peace of Prague, 1635

The Swedish invasion, 1630

The peace of Lubeck in May 1629 forced the Dutch and the French to look to Sweden as a replacement for Denmark in the Hague Coalition. By then Gustavus Adolphus was in a stronger position in the Baltic. Since the treaty of Stolbova in 1617, Sweden had gained control of the Baltic trade. Gustavus Adolphus had captured Livonia and Riga in 1621, in an attempt to reduce the power of King Sigismund of Poland–Lithuania. In 1626 he had advanced further into east Prussia and by 1629 had conquered Elbing, Memel and Pillau and enforced the neutrality of Danzig. To bring Sweden into the Coalition and to free her for action against the Habsburgs, the French mediated the truce of Altmark on 25 September 1629 between Sweden and Poland. Sweden gained Livonia and, more importantly, the administration of the Prussian customs.

At first France was limited in her negotiations with Sweden by the treaty of Regensburg concerning the Mantuan issue. By it France had undertaken not to ally with Ferdinand's enemies. This was a further reason for Richelieu's annoyance with his envoys. It was known that he had hoped to make an alliance with Gustavus, as well as to enlist Maximilian of Bavaria and the Catholic League as a major counter-weight to Habsburg power in Europe. The more favourable peace of Cherasco had not been arranged between the Emperor and the French when Gustavus Adolphus landed with his troops in Pomerania on 6 July 1630 (**155**). The French were forced into an alliance with Gustavus, against the terms of the Regensburg treaty, because they wanted to retain some influence over Swedish movements in Europe. However, Richelieu was clearly at a disadvantage, for he did not know what Gustavus would do or how powerful he would become.

The five-year agreement signed between France and Sweden at Bärwalde on 31 January 1631 provided Sweden with one million livres per annum (see Note, p. vi). In return for this French financial support, Gustavus promised to march into Germany to halt the run of defeats of the Coalition powers. [**doc 20**, ii]. Sweden was to protect the commercial interests of France, liberate the separate states of the Empire from Ferdinand's control, and be mindful of the neutrality of·Saxony and Bavaria. Neither France nor Sweden was to conclude a separate peace for the duration of the agreement. The treaty proved an embarrassment to France, since it portrayed her as an ally of a Protestant power [**doc. 5**].

On the other hand, Gustavus Adolphus soon realised that he was not welcome in north Germany, for only the Dukes of Pomerania and Mecklenburg and the Landgrave of Hesse–Cassel proved·co-operative [**doc. 12**]. John George of Saxony saw the Swedish invasion as a threat to 'German Liberties' and he managed to persuade an assembly of Protestant German states at Leipzig in March 1631 to support a 'Leipzig Manifesto' which made provision for raising an independent army. John George procured the services of one of Wallenstein's able generals, Hans George von Arnim, and it was soon clear that Sweden would have to compromise with this new force to prevent it from allying with the Catholic League.

In May 1631, before a formal alliance between Sweden, Saxony and Brandenburg could be arranged, the Catholic League army, under Tilly, captured Magdeburg and cruelly sacked and looted it [**doc. 13**]. This disaster aroused Protestant feeling throughout Europe. The United Provinces made a treaty with Sweden and agreed to provide subsidies, while Gustavus Adolphus marched to Berlin and forced the recalcitrant Duke of Brandenburg into an alliance. Gustavus then occupied Pomerania and conquered Mecklenburg, restoring the Dukes whom Wallenstein had dispossessed.

Tilly was not in a good position to retaliate. In May 1631 Maximilian of Bavaria had signed the treaty of Fontainebleau with France by which, in return for French recognition of his electoral title, Maximilian promised not to aid the enemies of France nor to attack her allies. Since the treaty of Bärwalde, Sweden had been an acknowledged ally of France, and Tilly therefore could not openly attack Gustavus Adolphus. However, partly to find resources for his army, and partly to punish John George for defying Imperial commands, Tilly invaded Saxony in September 1631 and took control of Leipzig. John George was forced to ask Gustavus for help and the Swedish and Saxon army defeated Tilly at Breitenfeld, just north of Leipzig on 17 September (**7** vol. II,·pp.

63–67). Tilly was forced to retreat towards Bavaria, Gustavus occupied the Lower Palatinate and the bishoprics of Wurzburg, Bamberg and Mainz, while the Saxons marched into Bohemia and captured Prague.

The speed and scale of the Swedish invasion alarmed Richelieu and many of the German Princes, especially Maximilian of Bavaria. In December 1631, in order to prevent mass defections of Princes from the anti-Habsburg cause, Richelieu offered French protection to any Prince who asked for it, though only the Elector of Trier responded. French troops were garrisoned at Philippsburg and Ehrenbreitsten, but this could not disguise the fact that Gustavus Adolphus was practically master of Germany and not as susceptible to French influence as Richelieu would have liked. Maximilian of Bavaria openly ignored French assurances that Bavaria was safe from Swedish attack and anxiously sought the Emperor's protection. He even called for the re-appointment of Wallenstein, and in December 1631 Ferdinand complied with his request.

Wallenstein insisted that his appointment should be for just three months in the first instance. At the end of that time he hoped to be in a stronger position to force on the Emperor more ambitious conditions for his continued service. His strategy succeeded and under the terms of a new agreement, made at Göllersdorf on 13 April 1632, he was promised regular subsidies for his troops from Ferdinand and Spain; he was given financial compensation for his help and confirmed in his dukedom of Mecklenburg; and he was authorised to negotiate peace with any Prince (though his dealings with Saxony had to be vetted by the Imperial Diet). The only major restriction was that he was not allowed to use the troops of the Catholic League or Spain without due permission.

Yet Wallenstein's appointment came too late to prevent Gustavus Adolphus from invading Bavaria and defeating the League army at Lech, in March 1632, mortally wounding the seventy-three-year-old Tilly in the process. The Swedes captured Augsburg and the Bavarian capital of Munich. Frederick V, who accompanied the Swedish army, looked to the future with renewed confidence as it appeared that his old titles and territories would soon be restored.

However, Swedish progress had been deceptively successful. Regensburg and Ingoldstadt held out against Gustavus and in May 1632 Wallenstein re-captured Prague, which allowed him to open negotiations with the Saxons. In order to prevent John George from breaking with the Swedes, Gustavus abandoned his advance towards Vienna and moved northwards to support the Saxons. It was now a time for taking stock, and in June 1632, after moving to Nuremburg, Gustavus Adolphus published revised plans for a settlement of the German question. They were based on the idea of creating two Protestant leagues – the *Corpus Bellicum* to be responsible for military affairs, and the *Corpus Evangelicorum* to take over civil administration. He wanted to preserve the existing structure of the states of the Empire and confirm toleration for Protestantism throughout Germany. He certainly did not envisage, at that stage, claiming the Imperial crown for himself. Territorially, he wanted to retain control of at least part of the south Baltic coast – from the Vistula to the Elbe – with Brandenburg being compensated with control of Silesia. This would have satisfied Sweden's *assecuratio* (security for the future), while the profits that would be gained from port revenues and increased trade would partly fulfil Swedish demands for *satisfactio* (compensation for Sweden's war-effort). However, these long-term aspirations were dependent on continued Swedish success, and the course of events now turned in the Emperor's favour.

Wallenstein had ensconced himself in the strong fortified position of the *Alte Feste* near Nuremberg and Gustavus was unable to move him. When Wallenstein finally turned northwards he easily captured Leipzig and forced Gustavus to follow him. The two armies met at Lützen, near Leipzig, on 16 November 1632. Wallenstein had to withdraw from the field and retreated into Bohemia, but there was no decisive victory. Sweden lost fifteen thousand troops and among the dead was Gustavus Adolphus himself. Bernard of Weimar and Axel Oxenstierna were thus suddenly left with the difficult task of maintaining Sweden's vulnerable possessions in Germany.

The Heilbronn League and the fall of Wallenstein

Why was there no general pacification after the battle of Lützen? John George of Saxony joined with Christian IV of Denmark in seeking to make peace with Ferdinand. Gustavus Adolphus' death had thwarted the hopes of the Bohemian exiles, as had the death of Frederick V in the same month. Even the Swedish government, with the young Queen Christina now at the helm, was considering the terms on which it would conclude a settlement. The reasons for

29

the failure to achieve a settlement are to be found in the diplomatic activity of Axel Oxenstierna and the military activity of Wallenstein.

Oxenstierna wanted to retain a strong Protestant Union as *assecuratio* against Habsburg power and to keep control of Pomerania as *satisfactio* for military services already rendered by Gustavus. He invited representatives of the Swabian, Franconian, Upper Rhenish and Electoral Circles, as well as John George of Saxony, to a meeting in Heilbronn in March 1633. Here he attempted to cement Gustavus' plans for a *Corpus Evangelicorum*. The result was the League of Heilbronn, established in April [**doc. 6**]. It did not include Saxony in the end, since John George once more supported the Emperor, but Richelieu accepted the idea of the League and, along with Sweden, France became a joint 'protector' of the new defensive organisation. It soon won a major victory, for in November 1633 Bernard of Weimar captured Regensburg.

Meanwhile, Wallenstein's activities also created tensions in Europe after the battle of Lützen. The Imperial commander made full use of the Göllersdorf Agreement to undertake negotiations for a separate peace with Saxony, but he also had secret negotiations with Sweden and France which lay outside the terms of the Agreement and this only served to increase the general mistrust of his aims. In October 1633 Wallenstein forced a Swedish army to capitulate at Steinau but then released the captured generals in return for some fortresses in Silesia held by Bohemian exiles. He also sent one of his generals, Aldringen, to Bavaria to supervise Swedish troop movements but with the express instructions not to engage the Swedes in battle, even though they captured Regensburg. In fact Aldringen became exasperated by Wallenstein's inactivity and, against orders, marched to relieve the besieged city of Breisach. This was an indication that there was growing opposition to Wallenstein not only at the Imperial court, but also amongst his own officer corps.

Historians have failed to agree on the rationale for Wallenstein's actions in 1633. Maland suggests that there was no coherent strategy: 'He was undeniably in a situation of tortuous complexity; he was also ageing rapidly, gouty and subject to fits of depression in which only his brother-in-law, Trcka, and Holk, his general, could approach him' (**26** p. 141). The French were certainly baffled by him, for as Feuquières lamented in 1633: 'His game is too subtle for me. From his silence in the face of all that I have offered him, I can only assume that what he really wants is strife between Your Majesty [Louis XIII] and his allies' (**29** p. 230 and **doc. 4**).

Wallenstein's critics at the Imperial Court finally persuaded the Emperor to issue orders for his arrest. Significantly, it was Ottavio Piccolomini, Wallenstein's principal lieutenant, who was given the job of organising his commander's downfall. Many other officers had gradually deserted Wallenstein, taking their troops with them, and when he retreated behind the walls of his fortress at Eger Wallenstein's command had been reduced to four generals and some 1,500 men. It was here that Piccolomini's band of English, Irish and Scots officers caught up with Wallenstein and assassinated him as he was about to go to bed. This time the Emperor had lost his *Generalissimo* for good.

The peace of Prague, 1635

The Imperial army was now commanded by the Emperor's son, the Archduke Ferdinand. He was married to the Spanish Infanta and had established links with her brother, the Cardinal–Infante, who had been nominated as governor of the Spanish Netherlands. Together, these two able men attempted to revive the alliance between the Spanish and Austrian Habsburgs and to reverse the advances made by Protestantism in the Empire. In 1634 their armies joined forces at Nördlingen and heavily defeated the Swedish army under Horn and Bernard of Weimar. South Germany once more passed into Habsburg control and the Heilbronn League seemed in disarray.

John George of Saxony submitted peace proposals towards the end of 1634 and a final peace was signed in Prague in May 1635. It remained open for other states to sign later if they cared to, and briefly the peace appeared the basis for a general settlement in central Europe. By it, the Edict of Restitution was repealed for a period of forty years, after which the Emperor was to be free to decide on the issues that it covered. In the meantime Lutherans were to retain those ecclesiastical possessions they held on 12 November 1627, but Calvinists were once again excluded from the arrangements. Protestant administrators of bishoprics were prevented from attending the Imperial Diet, since the 'ecclesiastical reservation' was to remain in force. There was to be an amnesty for all those who had fought against Ferdinand, although it was not to include the Bohemian exiles or the family of Frederick V. The

Palatinate remained Maximilian's, and the Dukes of Mecklenburg and Pomerania regained control of their respective territories. Alliances between the separate states of the Empire were to be forbidden; all armed forces were to be integrated into the Imperial army financed by the states but under the control of Imperial commissioners, and the Electors were only to command these troops as Imperial generals.

Though a number of members of the Heilbronn League refused to accept these terms, Ferdinand was relieved that Bavaria, Brandenburg, Saxony, Mainz, Cologne, Trier and other important principalities and cities did sign the peace. It made it possible for the Emperor to claim that the major Princes of the Empire were now united behind him and supported the old Imperial constitution based on 'German Liberties'.

4 The Entry of France and the Search for Peace

It is an indication of how far the Thirty Years War was not solely a German war that the peace of Prague failed to provide the basis for a general settlement. France, Sweden and the Netherlands had been alarmed at the possible consequences of a general peace arranged by the Emperor. The Swedes, though too poor and vulnerable to sustain indefinitely the kind of campaign waged by Gustavus Adolphus, nevertheless continued to fight in the hope of gaining territorial satisfaction. Yet they needed outside support. In April 1635 they concluded the treaty of Compiègne with the French in order to maintain their military commitments.

This treaty was yet another attempt by Richelieu to continue the struggle against the Habsburgs without formally declaring war. France had inadequate resources of men, money and commanders to sustain a prolonged series of campaigns. She controlled much of Lorraine and Alsace and in March 1635 her troops once more cut the Spanish Road when they overran the Valtelline. However, the Dutch had been anxious to get France directly involved in the war against Spain and were not content with the Franco–Dutch alliance of February 1635 by which France provided 30,000 men for the Dutch to re-deploy as they required. Fortunately for Sweden and the Dutch, Spanish troops marched into Trier and captured the Archbishop Elector who, since 1631, had been under French protection. This affront, coupled with the knowledge that Spain, the Emperor and the Catholic Princes of Germany had agreed at Ebersdorf in October 1634 on a joint attack on France, led Louis XIII to declare war on Spain on 19 May 1635.

French troops were poorly disciplined and inexperienced and Richelieu was forced to seek alliances with sympathetic powers. In July 1635 he signed a treaty with Savoy, Parma and Mantua for a joint campaign in northern Italy. In October he took Bernard of Weimar and his army into French service. However, the achievement of his aims depended on a radical improvement in the state of French finances. Richelieu therefore raised loans, sold offices, and placed Intendants on permanent location in the French provinces to ensure the collection of taxes.

Meanwhile the Spaniards drove the French out of the Valtelline and then, in 1636, the Habsburg powers attempted a series of lightning manoeuvres against France itself. The Cardinal–Infante and Piccolomini were to attack through Picardy while another Imperial army under Gallas pushed through the Vosges Gap from the east and Philip IV of Spain led an invading army from the south.

The Cardinal–Infante pushed forward as far as Compiègne, but the French stiffened their resistance and would not allow the Spaniards to take Paris. Gallas was prevented from joining the Cardinal–Infante by Bernard, while Philip IV's assault from the south failed to materialise. The Cardinal–Infante was eventually forced to retreat, but the prestige of France had been dented. This was demonstrated further in the autumn of 1636 when the Electors, meeting once again at Regensburg, disregarded French advice and agreed to Ferdinand's request that his son should be elected King of the Romans. However, in February 1637 Ferdinand died and his son succeeded him as Ferdinand III.

The new Emperor needed to establish his authority and standing with the Princes of the Empire, but circumstances were unfavourable for him. The military balance tilted against the Habsburg cause. The Swedes, under Baner and Torstensson, recovered their pride and morale and in October 1636 defeated a combined Saxon and Imperial force at Wittstock in Brandenburg. Sweden soon controlled much of northern Germany – a state of affairs which compelled Gallas to abandon his attack on France. However, Baner was defeated by Gallas at Torgau and the Swedes were once more forced back into Pomerania. Oxenstierna had to negotiate the treaty of Hamburg with the French (March 1638) in order to gain sufficient financial support to keep the Swedish army operational. This support allowed the Swedes to recover their morale and in 1639 they marched into Bohemia.

Bernard of Weimar was also active in 1638 and he defeated Imperial troops at Rheinfelden on the Rhine. This allowed the French to push on to Breisach which was successfully besieged by the able French commander, Turenne. Once again the Spanish Road was severed. Bernard then occupied Alsace and claimed it for himself. This embarrassed Richelieu, but fortunately for France Bernard died in July 1639 and his army was brought directly under the control of French commanders.

The United Provinces had been relieved when France declared war. They had recovered Schenkenschans in 1636 and in 1637 Frederick Henry recaptured Breda. But the success at Breda could not prevent objections to the costly war. Dutch Regents (merchant oligarchs) were opposed to extra involvement in Europe. For them, naval exploits in the New World appeared more lucrative, and their view was given a boost by the defeat of a Spanish armada by Tromp at the battle of the Downs in October 1639. The defeat of a flotilla of Spanish and Portuguese ships near Pernambuco in January 1640 added further support for their view. Yet despite these differences of opinion, the Dutch government was anxious that the Franco–Spanish conflict should continue. Meanwhile the Cardinal–Infante held off the Dutch army as best he could, but he died in November 1641, and this merely compounded the misfortunes that had befallen Spain. The Dutch now sensed victory.

The battle of the Downs had cut Spain's sea route with Flanders and increased the mounting pressures on Olivares' government in Madrid. The project of the Union of Arms had failed to get much response from the other four kingdoms of the Spanish monarchy, and the *almirantazgo* policy had not forced the Dutch to surrender. When the French invaded Rousillon in 1639 Catalonia suddenly became vulnerable and needed to be defended. However, the Catalans refused voluntarily to raise men and money for this purpose and in 1640 Castilian troops were sent to do the job for them. Yet these troops were poorly paid and had to live off the land, and their behaviour sparked off a full-scale revolt. The Catalans sought help from France, and in January 1641 a joint French–Catalan army defeated the Castilians outside Barcelona (**98**).

Olivares also faced trouble in Portugal in 1640. Late in the year the Duke of Braganza led a revolt to support his claim to the throne and prevent Castile's centralising policies from undermining the rights and privileges of the Portuguese nobility. In December 1640 Braganza proclaimed himself John IV of Portugal. In January 1641 his brother-in-law, Medina Sidonia, attempted to take control of Andalusia and assert its independence. Although he was unsuccessful, Sidonia's action was yet another indication that the Spanish monarchy was threatened with disintegration from within. Olivares clearly needed a major success. He hoped that Philip IV's campaign to crush the Catalans in mid-1642 would stem the run of defeats, but it did not. In January 1643 he was dismissed as chief minister and soon afterwards died.

However France was not in a position to capitalise on this turn of events. Richelieu had died on 4 December 1642, to be followed by Louis XIII on 14 May 1643. Since the new King, Louis XIV, was only four years old, the Queen Mother, Anne of Austria, led a Council of Regency supported by the Italian, Giulio Mazzarini – better known as Mazarin. The Spaniards hoped to gain a dominant influence over this Council and, although they failed to do so, the pressures Spain brought to bear on France temporarily prevented Mazarin from adopting a more aggressive stance in Europe.

Even before Louis XIII's death, Don Francisco de Melo, successor to the Cardinal–Infante, had invaded France and had to be defeated by Condé at Rocroi in May 1643. Then the Spaniards tried to exploit a conspiracy of nobles led by Vendome and the Duchess of Chevreuse – the 'importants' – but this led to nothing. With France unable to mount a serious campaign in Europe while these internal difficulties persisted, the exhausting military deadlock there could not be broken.

Throughout Europe there was a longing for peace after 1640, but none of the belligerents was prepared to sacrifice hard-won gains or surrender unachieved ambitions without adequate compensation. The French and Swedes had already agreed, in the treaty of Hamburg of 1638, that although they would each continue to seek satisfactory territorial concessions in any peace negotiations, in principle there ought to be a return to the *status quo* of 1618.

The new Emperor, Ferdinand III, wished to retain the Imperial gains made at the peace of Prague, which meant using the year 1627 as the base-date for negotiations on territorial distribution. However, the Electors preferred 1618 and favoured the Franco–Swedish proposals. Ferdinand summoned a Diet to Regensburg in September 1640 in an attempt to preserve the peace of Prague, but he did not succeed. The Elector of Brandenburg died in October and his successor, Frederick William, the Great Elector, was quick to denounce the peace of Prague as a basis for a general European settlement. In July 1641 he made a separate truce with Sweden. This unilateral arrangement acted as a catalyst for other German Princes seeking to oppose the Emperor's policies. Ferdinand III dissolved the Diet in October 1641 with little accomplished. He had already been making arrangements for holding separate peace meetings with the French and Dutch at Münster, and the Swedes at Osnabrück, and the German Princes were anxious to be involved in the new negotiations.

However, in 1642, in order to gain a strong bargaining position at Osnabrück, the Swedes swept into Moravia and Saxony and defeated the Imperial forces at the second battle of Breitenfeld. The French also maintained a military threat after the battle of Rocroi, but it was not until July 1645 that Condé won another major victory at the second battle of Nördlingen. When the Swedes, in the same year, defeated the Imperial forces at Jankau, the Habsburgs finally realised that they could not win the war. Yet it was equally clear that neither France nor Sweden was in a position to press forward to a total victory. In fact Sweden had been forced into a war with Denmark and her fleet had been defeated near Kolberg Heath.

In 1645 the Swedes signed the treaty of Bromsebro with Denmark and gained Gotland, Osel and the provinces of Jemteland and Herjedalen, as well as exemption from the Sound dues. Queen Christina also concluded a separate peace with Saxony at Katschenbroda in September (**199**).

Thus by 1646 Ferdinand III was in a precarious position. He had lost Brandenburg and Saxony; in addition he could not rely on Bavaria's loyalty, he felt threatened once more in Hungary and he could not really expect much help from Spain. In the circumstances he felt compelled to send his chief administrator, Trautmansdorf, to Westphalia to finalise peace arrangements. Even so the fighting continued. In 1647 French and Swedish forces forced Maximilian of Bavaria to abandon his alliance with Ferdinand III, and when he reneged on this Maximilian's territories were devastated. In August 1648, Ferdinand's brother Leopold, Governor of the Netherlands, was heavily defeated by the French at Lens at the same time as the Swedes were besieging Prague. Thus, throughout the period of negotiations at Münster and Osnabrück, the military pressure on the Habsburgs was intensified.

The French eventually got Ferdinand to agree to exclude the Spanish from the general peace arrangements but this did not prevent the United Provinces and Spain from signing a ceasefire at Münster in June 1647. The peace arrangements were finalised in the treaty of Münster on 30 January 1648. Much to Mazarin's annoyance – for Spain would now be free to concentrate on her war with France – the Eighty Years War between Spain and the rebel United Provinces had come to an end.

This hardened the attitude of both France and Sweden in favour of negotiating a withdrawal from the European war. Both countries gained Ferdinand's agreement that the practice of electing a King of the Romans in an Emperor's lifetime (in order to secure a *de facto*

Habsburg successor) should be abolished. More importantly, Ferdinand had to concede that the Empire would remain neutral in the war between France and Spain, and that this was to hold even if Franche-Comté, a member of the Diet, was involved. The treaties of Münster and Osnabrück, collectively known as the peace of Westphalia, were finally ratified by the participating governments in February 1649 [**doc. 8**].

Summary of the peace arrangements and some consequences

THE EMPIRE

By the peace of Westphalia the separate states of the Empire were recognised as independent members of the Imperial Diet, free to control their own affairs. The principle of *cuius regio, eius religio* was reaffirmed, which could have had dire consequences in some areas but, because of princely toleration, did not. The Edict of Restitution, temporarily in abeyance from 1635, was finally withdrawn and, except for Austria and Bavaria, 1624 was stipulated as the base year for calculating which secularised lands could be retained. Calvinism was now brought within the provisions of the 1555 settlement of Augsburg and religious disputes were to be settled by compromise rather than by majority decisions in the Diet. Maximilian was finally granted the Upper Palatinate with its electoral title, and he managed to retain the bishoprics of Paderborn and Osnabrück for his family. Charles Louis, the eldest son of Frederick V, was allowed to control the Lower Palatinate and a new electoral title (the eighth) was created for him. Saxony was allowed to retain Lusatia. The arrangements at Cherasco in 1631, whereby the Duke of Nevers gained Mantua, Montferrat and Casale, were now confirmed.

Frederick William of Brandenburg acquired most territory from the peace arrangements. His possession of Cleves, Mark and Ravensberg – previously agreed in the treaty of Xanten in 1614 – was confirmed, and he also came to control eastern Pomerania and the important bishoprics of Minden, Cammin and Halberstadt. He was also promised Magdeburg when the existing administrator died. Admittedly Frederick William had to give up 6,500 square kilometres of land, but he received 9,500 in compensation.

The Emperor himself established his hereditary rights in Moravia, Silesia and Bohemia, though he had to cede the Sundgau to France. The attempts to cement Habsburg authority in the Empire

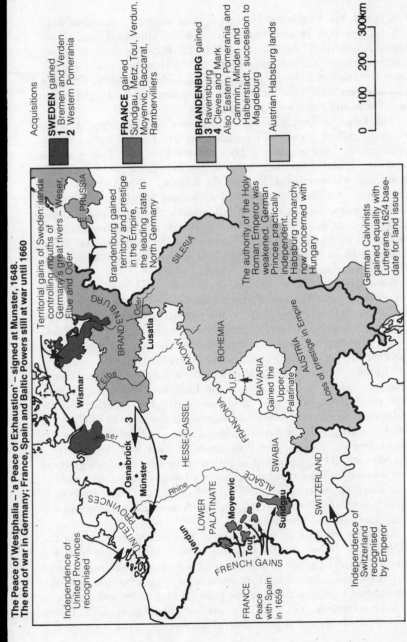

The Peace of Westphalia – 'a Peace of Exhaustion' – signed at Munster, 1648.
The end of war in Germany; France, Spain and Baltic Powers still at war until 1660

Acquisitions

SWEDEN gained
1 Bremen and Verden
2 Western Pomerania

FRANCE gained
Sundgau, Metz, Toul, Verdun, Moyenvic, Baccarat, Rambervilliers

BRANDENBURG gained
3 Ravensburg
4 Cleves and Mark
Also Eastern Pomerania and Cammin, Minden and Halberstadt, succession to Magdeburg

Austrian Habsburg lands

Territorial gains of Sweden: lands controlling mouths of Germany's great rivers – Weser, Elbe and Oder

Brandenburg gained territory and prestige in the Empire, the leading state in North Germany

The authority of the Holy Roman Emperor was weakened. German Princes practically independent. Habsburg monarchy now concerned with Hungary

German Calvinists gained equality with Lutherans. 1624 base-date for land issue

Independence of United Provinces recognised

Independence of Switzerland recognised by Emperor

FRANCE Peace with Spain in 1659

FRENCH GAINS

BAVARIA Gained the Upper Palatinate

Loss of prestige

0   100   200   300km

had failed, but Ferdinand III had at least succeeded in strengthening his position in the 'hereditary lands'. Though Hungary remained unsettled, Ferdinand could still hope to have a strong barrier against Turkish aspirations in the Danube area. He managed to retain the word 'German' as part of his Imperial title, but his interests were now focused on the eastern part of the Empire and Habsburg links with Hungary were to grow (**22**).

The Imperial Diet was still divided into three 'colleges' and the electoral college preserved its predominance. The Elector of Mainz retained the Directory of the Diet and the Elector of Bohemia was again excluded from the electoral union because he was also a King and indistinguishable from the Emperor. The German Princes achieved a form of territorial autonomy which, to all intents and purposes, was as good as full sovereignty. They could negotiate and conclude treaties with other countries, providing they did not direct alliances against the Emperor or the 'public peace' of the Empire. Thus 'German Liberties', as defined by the 'states and Princes' were safeguarded.

Although freedom of worship was permitted, it was not actually established in 1648. The Princes alone were free to choose their faith and, in theory, impose it on their subjects. Only where a ruler changed his religion were his subjects free to retain theirs. Thus where freedom of private worship was allowed, this was only through the personal tolerance of the individual Prince.

The peace arrangements also settled the future of those Princes who had taken up arms against the Emperor, and most of them had their possessions and lands returned. The solution to the Palatinate problem had involved increasing the number of electoral titles to eight, with the balance tilted in favour of the Catholics. To avoid trouble, each of the Protestants in turn was later given a double vote (**31** p. 236). The question of the peace treaty's guarantee, whereby all the contracting powers became guarantors, meant that Germany was not in full control of her fortunes. Indeed, it meant that any internal German problem could still be infused with international significance.

Although the Princes of the Empire had gained more say in the direction of Imperial affairs, to the outside observer in 1650 the map of central Europe still resembled a confusing kaleidoscope of autonomous Catholic and Protestant states. To a large extent, the settlements merely confirmed the political and religious fragmentation of Germany. Yet they also marked the beginning of a long period of greater stability in central Europe.

SWEDEN

Queen Christina finally settled for five million thalers (see Note, p. vi) as Sweden's *satisfactio*, and her *assecuratio* ensured Swedish domination of practically the entire North German coastline. Sweden controlled the mouths of the Elbe, Oder and Weser and occupied western Pomerania, Stettin, Wismar and Stralsund. The dioceses of Bremen and Verden, and the islands of Rügen, Usedom and Wollin were also under Swedish control. Swedish acquisitions made in the treaty of Bromsebro in 1645 were confirmed. Christina demanded that 1618 should be the base-year for settling the religious and political affairs of Europe. Although this was rejected in favour of 1624, the settlement was seen by many people at the time as a great victory for the Swedish Queen.

However, the years immediately following the 1648 peace were very anxious ones for Christina. The continuation of the war after Gustavus Adolphus' death had been financed at the expense of the royal estates through the conversion of rents in kind for cash. A few unscrupulous noble families came to own lands worth about one–fifth of the kingdom's revenues. Not surprisingly, the government ran short of money and sought the *Riksdag*'s approval to levy indirect taxes. The peasants refused, many having already been severely treated by their new noble landlords. The clergy and townsmen supported the peasants in seeking a reduction in government spending. They demanded that the crown should recover lost lands, and as this seemed unlikely, they refused to accept the tax proposals (**194**).

In 1650, after a poor harvest, the *Riksdag* met for four months and the tenor of the speeches scared the leading Swedish nobles. They needed Christina's support and were forced to accept Charles Gustav as hereditary Prince to placate her. He became King Charles X in 1654 when Christina abdicated (to become a Catholic). Contrary to the nobles' expectation, Charles attempted only a limited *reduktion* (recovery) of crown lands, which pleased nobody. On a general level he sought to unite Sweden by going to war with Poland in 1655. Although Charles was not entirely successful in this venture, by the treaty of Roskilde of 1658 Sweden gained Halland and forced Denmark to give up Skane and therefore control of the Sound. The treaty effectively established the territorial framework of modern Sweden.

However, peace forced Charles to face the social pressures that he thought the war would have alleviated. He could not afford to disband his army and so decided to fight Denmark, on the grounds of her unwillingness to close the Sound to Dutch ships. He soon came to realise, however, that the Danes, who had French, English and Dutch support, could not be beaten. Yet he did not dare terminate hostilities. These were ended only after his death in 1660, when, by the treaty of Copenhagen, Sweden abandoned her attempts to close the Sound. A conference at Oliva, involving Sweden, France, Austria and other concerned powers, agreed that Poland should acquire the southern part of Livonia in return for renouncing any claim on the Swedish throne; that Frederick William should gain confirmation of his sovereignty in Prussia; and that Russia should confirm Sweden's possession of the Baltic provinces. Thus the peace of Westphalia had not settled the conflicts in the Baltic, though it had established Sweden as the predominant power there. Yet by 1660 Sweden's status as a major imperial power was clearly threatened. By 1718 the Swedish imperial experience would almost be at an end (**194** p.1).

FRANCE

Mazarin managed to secure possession of Breisach and Philippsburg as well as the Sundgau, thereby increasing French control of the bishoprics of Metz, Toul and Verdun (originally gained in 1559), and France's influence in Lorraine. Yet the peace did not settle the problem of Lorraine. Lorraine had been recognised as independent by Charles V in 1542, but in 1648 the French were reluctant to evacuate it and the issue remained a problem for France even after the treaty of the Pyrenees of 1659 was thought to have settled it.

France became one of the guarantors of the 1648 settlement and as such acquired a right to watch over the Empire's internal affairs, with authority to intervene if she thought the general peace might be threatened.

It is customary to record that after 1648 France's ascendancy in Europe was assured. However, with serious problems at home, it was not at all clear that France was in a position to exploit the disadvantages facing the other powers. The war with Spain continued until the treaty of the Pyrenees in 1659, and during that time there had been fears that Cromwell would help Spain in return for gaining control of Calais and Bordeaux. France never felt strong enough to fight alone and Mazarin was constantly seeking allies. She was not strong enough to influence the Imperial election in 1658 when, despite large cash inducements, the Estates elected a Habsburg (Leopold) as Ferdinand's successor (**14**).

SPAIN

Not only was Spain embarrassed by the revolts in Portugal, Catalonia and Naples (1647); she was also humiliated by being excluded from the general Westphalian settlement. Mazarin secured Imperial neutrality in the Franco–Spanish conflict and increased French influence in Alsace and Lorraine. Spain was even deprived of her Rhineland bases. However, Philip IV managed to secure maritime supremacy in the Mediterranean and recaptured Barcelona in 1652. French involvement in the Catalan revolt came to an end and by 1656 Mazarin was on the point of seeking peace. Yet, given the hostility of England and the neutrality of the Rhineland Princes, Philip IV had to sign the treaty of the Pyrenees in 1659, by which he gave up Rousillon and Perpignan and recognised all French gains made in 1648. Spanish fortresses along the eastern French border were also removed.

The Catalan revolt came to an end in 1659, but the Portuguese issue continued to trouble Spain. The Portuguese had regained Brazil from the Dutch in 1654 and the trading profits allowed them to fight on for independence from Spain. They defeated Spanish forces at Elvas in 1658 and actually invaded Spain, laying siege to Badajoz. From 1661 they gained the help of Charles II of England and eventually, in 1668, Spain was forced to recognise Portugal's independence.

Thus at the end of almost a century of war, Spain could point only to a string of bankruptcies and humiliations. The United Provinces and Portugal had been lost; Andalusia and Catalonia threatened to become other Portugals; and Seville had risen in revolt, marking a new age of popular protest in the Peninsula. Yet at least up to 1656, as Stradling says '...no more than in France or England were ... calamities, either individually or collectively, of a strength sufficient to destroy the fabric of the state, even one so peculiar and precarious as the Spanish monarchy' (**201** p. 142).

THE UNITED PROVINCES

By the treaty of Münster, the United Provinces gained their independence not only from Spain but also from the Holy Roman Empire. They did not have to concede guarantees concerning the rights of Roman Catholics and were allowed to retain their conquests in the Spanish Netherlands and overseas. Though Antwerp remained blockaded, the Dutch were allowed to trade freely in the East and West Indies.

Even so, in the years immediately following the settlement there was the threat of civil war in the United Provinces. William II had wanted to keep the House of Orange in the forefront of European politics by allying with France against Spain. The Estates of Holland, heavily in debt, demanded that the army be reduced and economies made. William tried to frighten the Estates into maintaining their high taxes and he persuaded the *Stadtholder* of Friesland to attack Amsterdam.

Though William died before the English civil war broke out, the Dutch were involved in a conflict with England after the Commonwealth passed the Navigation Act in 1651. It was a naval war and came at a time when the Dutch needed time to consolidate their republic. The treaty of Westminster in 1654 was not to be a sound basis for peace, and a second Anglo–Dutch war broke out in 1666. Although the Dutch were victorious, their 'Golden Age' after 1648 was clearly not a period devoid of tensions and anxieties. England came to replace Spain as a serious trading rival and France threatened to replace Spanish hegemony in Europe.

The Westphalian settlements: a turning point?

Although the Westphalian Agreements did not actually end war in Europe, the territorial changes made in 1648 remained formally valid until the nineteenth century, despite many minor alterations. Although religion continued to be intricately bound up with decisions of state, its influence on internal affairs was less obvious after 1648; the provision that 1624 was to be the standard year for reservation of ecclesiastical property meant that further religious dissension like that of Donauworth in 1608 did not recur and the assumption that territory had to be reclaimed for one side or the other was gradually abandoned. The territorial distribution of the main religions, with Lutheranism entrenched in the northern part of the Empire, Calvinism important in the Rhine area and Catholicism dominant in the south, remained intact until the twentieth century.

After 1648 there were more secure constitutional guarantees for both Catholic and Protestant Princes and the Imperial Diet did not disintegrate as it had done in 1608. When Louis XIV threatened to combine dynastic ambitions with old religious divisions in 1686, he was opposed by both Catholic and Protestant Princes allied together in the League of Augsburg, and it is significant that this League also comprised Spain, the Emperor, the Netherlands,

Sweden and England. To that extent, the treaty of Westphalia had established a relatively settled structure for conducting international affairs and, until the late eighteenth century, it was considered to be an important basis of the European state system.

Although there were many territorial changes made after 1648 (eg the treaty of Utrecht in 1713, which ceded many of Spain's possessions in Europe to Austria), the method of settling international disputes by congresses, backed by the signatories as 'guarantors', had been born. It was a reflection of the rare complexity of the conflicts of the previous thirty years that, after 1648, people began to believe that the Westphalian settlements had, after all, been a diplomatic turning point (**36**).

Part Three: Analysis

5: Economic and Social Effects of The Thirty Years War

The economic and social history of Europe in the first half of the seventeenth century is a minefield of conflicting interpretations and debates. There has been a lot of material on the theme of 'crisis', but no firm conclusions as to what sort of crisis actually existed, or whether the very concept of crisis is of any use to historians of the period (**127**). This division of opinion is reflected in two debates – whether the European economy suffered a decline in the first half of the seventeenth century, and what effects the Thirty Years War had on economic and social developments.

Some historians, like Chaunu, commenting on international trade (**86**), and Goubert, who has looked at a region in France, have used a study of prices to indicate that the European economy was in a depression by 1650, having shown many signs of retardation before that. Goubert thinks that war had only a peripheral economic and social significance, with local and temporary effects on prices. In his view, bad harvests were far more important, so that if there was a crisis, it was a 'subsistence crisis' (**104**).

Slicher van Bath, concerned more with agricultural production than price trends, also sees the mid-seventeeth century as the turning point into depression, with falling cereal prices, higher real wages and some increase in rural industry (**144**). Romano, however, has tried to link prices, monetary factors, trade and general production in a thesis which proposes the period 1619–22 as being the crucial turning point into recession (**138**). Baehrel and Le Roy Ladurie (**72**, **123**), basing their conclusions on particular regions, think that there was no real break in trends before 1650, although Le Roy Ladurie thinks there were some crises before then produced by the fiscal pressures arising from war. Marxist historians tend to view the first half of the seventeenth century as a period of economic stagnation and regard the Thirty Years War as assisting, though not initiating, structural changes from feudalism to capitalism.

This lack of agreement about general economic trends in seventeenth-century Europe has not been eased by more detailed studies of the effects of the war on Germany. This is because historians studying the economic and social condition of Germany in the seventeenth century have had to face the problems of generalising from wide regional variations and it is not therefore surprising that there have been disagreements about the impact of war. T. K. Rabb (**134**) has reviewed the debate between the two major 'schools' – the 'disastrous war school' who argue that the war brought a decline to the German economy, and the 'earlier decline school' who argue that the evil reputation of the war may have been exaggerated and that there was already a decline in many aspects of the economy prior to 1618. Rabb concludes that the 'earlier decline school' has only established that there was a decline in certain aspects relative to some European nations, leaving the question of the absolute condition of the German economy still open: 'From a condition of at worst, diversity, Germany had [after 1618] sunk into a situation dominated by decline.... At best, the Thirty Years War started a general decline that had not previously existed; at worst it replaced prosperity with disaster' (**134** p. 51).

H. Kamen has argued that to some extent this controversy over the condition of Germany is a false one. At the time, there was no single economic or political unit called 'Germany', rather a number of economies such that 'It is not possible to speak of the decline of Germany, but only of the decline of certain selected areas of Germany, some of which may have suffered from long-term factors of decay, while others were directly and physically annhilated by war' (**115**, p. 45). The very exercise of attempting to distinguish between pre-war decline and war-time decline tends, in his view, to minimise the destructive effects of the war and establish a simplistic categorisation which is inflexible with regard to evaluating processes that were both antedating and yet aggravated by war.

H. Kellenbenz has suggested that for the period 1500–1800 (**117** ch. 7) there were four broad regions within the Empire which possessed a common economic structure: the Rhine valley in the west; the coastal areas from Friesland to Prussia in the north; 'High Germany' with textile and metallurgical industries and international trading interests in the south; and central east Germany with a mining and metallurgical industry of growing importance. Before the war economic activity in these areas was increasing rapidly, with new land being brought into cultivation, rising population and increased production in almost all sectors. The war tended to end expansion in most regions and the resulting recession was prolonged by the import of goods from the rest of

Europe, by the exhaustion of many mines, by the shortage of fuel and by the high taxes on trade, tolls and customs dues. Although people learned to live with the demands of war, and although a loss or decline for one area may have been a gain or rise for another, Kellenbenz thinks that in 1650 Germany as a whole was less prosperous than it had been in 1550. With the Elbe as a dividing line, it is possible to say that after 1648 the western areas were more prosperous than the eastern ones. However, even within quite small areas on both sides there were pockets of prosperity existing alongside pockets of depression. Thus for Germany, and also for the rest of Europe, the concepts of 'economic advance' and 'economic decline' are difficult if not impossible to define, as the following examination of the main economic indicators reveals.

Population

In general terms, the population of Germany increased in the sixteenth century and then fell between 1600 and 1650 with a slow recovery between 1650 and 1700. The relevant figures are: 12 million in 1550, 15 million in 1600, 14 million in 1625, 11 million in 1650 and 15 million in 1700 (**152** ch. 7). War affected sections of the German people selectively. Rural areas suffered most, with losses to domestic and farm buildings, farming land and animals. Langer quotes figures that purport to show that the Swedish armies alone destroyed or seriously damaged about 2,000 castles, 18,000 villages and 1,500 towns – about one-third of all towns in Germany (**23** p. 8). Many municipal tax records indicate an increase in the number of 'deserted places' and villagers often fled at the approach of soldiers. Magdeburg at the beginning of the war had about 20–26,000 inhabitants and some 35,000 refugees from surrounding areas. By 1635, following Tilly's destruction in 1631, there remained only 394 households, and even by 1644 the population was still only 2,464.

Some demographic historians argue that urban areas in Germany lost one-third of their population and rural areas about 40 per cent, allowing for variations from less than 10 per cent in Lower Saxony to over 50 per cent in Württemberg and Pomerania. In many towns the birth rate fell below pre-war levels: in Stuttgart it fell by 48 per cent, in Augsburg 42 per cent, in Nuremberg 36 per cent. Yet the fact that Augsburg actually grew during the war period highlights one of the difficulties of handling population data. Urban statistics can be regarded as only approximate. In the seventeenth century it was not obligatory to keep parish registers, and tax returns, though helpful, are fragmentary. Even local censuses, where they exist, cannot be trusted entirely (**139** pp. 4–5).

However, Germany's demographic record is not unique. Few states in Europe experienced an increase in population in the seventeenth century as the following table (from **29** p. 23) indicates:

Year	1550	1575	1600	1625	1650	1675	1700
Bohemia			4	3	2.25		
England & Wales	3		4	4.5		5.8	5.8
France		20					19.3
Italy	11	13	13	13	12	11.5	12.5
Low Countries	3	3		3.5			4
Poland			8				8
Russia	9		11	8	9.5	13	16
Spain	6.3		7.6		5.2		7
All Europe	85	95	100	100	80	90	100

(*Figures in millions*)

Both in Germany and Europe generally, the worst demographic catastrophes occurred when the main scourges of famine, pestilence and war came together. There was a great plague outbreak in Germany in the years 1634–39. Frankfurt alone lost nearly 7,000 inhabitants in 1634 and in the years 1632–35 Augsburg lost nearly 18,000 [**doc. 16**]. The plague was endemic in Europe too up to 1665–66, with an epidemic once every fifteen years on average between the Black Death (in Europe 1347–50) and 1670. Even so, one of the great bouts of famine in Europe occurred in 1628–30 after a major extension of the fighting. Foreign armies were notorious for carrying disease. They were also a drain on local food supplies and a stimulant to inflation.

Obviously, a population's health was closely tied to the availability of food, but it has proved difficult to measure the direct effect of famine on population size. Most parish registers, particularly in Germany, attributed deaths to various infectious diseases rather than to starvation. Poor harvests and bad weather often brought misery, especially to areas dependent on a single-product economy. Yet the effects of bad weather might last only two years without recovery, whereas the effects of war could have longer-lasting repercussions, even to the extent of modifying a region's pattern of economic growth.

The term 'population loss', therefore, is deceptive and should not be equated with actual loss of life. Many people who abandoned their homes at the approach of an army may have returned later or increased the population of more peaceful areas. The actual area of devastation caused by armies was quite restricted. Although it is difficult to deny that the communities in the war corridors of the main military transit routes suffered terribly at various times during the Thirty Years War, it is also clear that physical destruction was sometimes short-lived. Rural areas often led the way in economic recovery, but Leipzig – which was besieged many times – continued to hold its annual trade fair and became a major centre of commerce, while Magdeburg had been rebuilt by the end of the war. Thus the older interpretation which depicts the war as a great scourge reducing large areas of central Europe to a wilderness is not universally applicable. However, famine, plunder, persecution and emigration caused genuine human suffering in many areas, and war often intensified and prolonged the misery.

Agriculture and peasantry

Analysis of agricultural trends in the seventeenth century has to rely on studies of prices or yield ratios, both of which have their disadvantages. Cooper has pointed out that 'price series, especially when presented as index numbers, silver equivalents, or moving averages, remain the basis for acts of faith rather than quantitative evidence about the development of the economy' (**16** p. 10). Even so it is possible to say that the Thirty Years War brought increased prices which lasted in Germany and Holland until the 1630s, in Italy until the 1620s and in the southern Netherlands, Austria and England until the 1640s. Prices then generally remained low until the eighteenth century (**135**, IV, pp. 86–7).

Yield ratios, as calculated by Slicher van Bath (**143**), suggest a decline in Germany post-1550 and again in the first half of the seventeenth century. In England, France and eastern Europe there was a decline in the first half of the seventeenth century and again in the second half. Although there was only a marked reduction in the export of corn from the Baltic region after the middle of the seventeenth century (**87**), this must be balanced by the fact that new crops like maize, rice and buckwheat were increasingly being cultivated to replace the highly priced grain. In the Netherlands, land reclamation was increasing until 1639, but between 1640 and 1660 this process declined (**16** p. 91). Beyond this, there are few statistics to determine decreases or increases in general production, or land reclamation, or to assess the balance between cereal cultivation and cattle rearing. Thus an exact turning point for European agricultural production cannot be identified.

However, during the war the consolidation of estates increased, and this had implications for the peasantry. The worst areas for estate consolidation were in Mecklenburg and Pomerania, but generally Princes were wary of the process since it served to increase the power of the nobility at their expense. Yet so anxious were the territorial sovereigns to restore their lands that they supported many ordinances giving the lords greater power over their peasants. Labour was scarce in many eastern areas after 1648 and lords were quick to exploit their legal position to bind their remaining peasants to the land, even if it meant increasing peasant wages. These rights over the peasants derived from the possession of land and were owed to the lord alone. Manorial domains were often like states within states and peasants were treated as part of the estates.

There were wide varieties of obligations. In East Prussia in the early seventeenth century there were many families owing labour services. Peasants on crown land usually fared better than those working for noble owners, who generally thought more in terms of production and profit (especially those involved in the corn trade of north-east Germany). Those peasants on holdings too small to provide tax revenue were worst off, having to give the heaviest services, often in commercial enterprises and manufacturing ventures developed by their lords.

Evans has shown how, after 1570, there was a major clash of interests between nobles and peasants in Habsburg lands which was especially marked in the period 1600–50 (**100**). The high demand for agricultural products in the sixteenth century had brought relative prosperity to some peasants (especially in Bohemia), but new commercial opportunities in wheat, wine, fish, cattle and sheep led to a change in direction of entrepreneurship by the nobles at a time when their returns from manorial dues were declining. Landowners were forced to safeguard their positions. Some relied on estate management by attempting to raise yields and use trained bailiffs, as in brewing and distilling, which often led to the purchase of peasant holdings. Others enforced 'robot' or extra compulsory services, which were often accompanied by higher payments in kind.

Historians of eastern Europe are wary of interpreting these practices as the development of a 'second serfdom'. In the east there was certainly a rise in agricultural prices which led to increased exploitation of the soil at a time when depopulation and war threatened an economic crisis. Yet landlord proprietors tended to profit by selling in foreign markets (especially by exporting grain via Danzig), and although this called for closer control of the peasantry the added element of commercial capitalism makes it difficult to equate these seventeenth-century developments with feudal practices of earlier periods.

In northern and western Europe, by contrast, serfdom had practically disappeared, especially where industry had expanded and where towns had increased in size. Commerce had begun to rival agriculture as a source of wealth and a way of life. The Thirty Years War did not initiate these processes, but it certaintly encouraged them. Indeed, had the Habsburgs been more successful in Europe, many areas would have developed differently. A Habsburg absolutism – with its own version of the Counter-Reformation – would have imposed a form of orthodoxy and suspicion of innovation which would have held back certain economic developments in the west. To that extent, the treaty of Westphalia marked the triumph of a more capitalistically oriented view of life and society over a more economically backward one. However, these are wide generalisations, and they need to be handled with care.

Industrial production

In Germany there was no central institution to take charge of 'industrial' data, and historians have had to rely on the records of towns and Princes who were interested enough in trade regulation and taxation to keep relevant figures, as well as on the records left by individual entrepreneurs. Much industry, other than mining and metallurgy, was based on the domestic 'putting out' system, where raw materials were distributed to workers in their homes. This was especially the case with textile production, which took place in most German towns. Lower Saxony, Hesse and Silesia were known for their linen, and Cologne for its silk, but diversity has defeated the attempts to compile total textile production figures for Germany.

Regional variation is also evident in general European textile production and it is not possible to draw any firm conclusions on the basis of local statistics. The Italian and Castilian data indicate a decline in the early years of the seventeenth century (**89, 142**); the statistics for English cloth suggest that 1614 was a crucial year and that after 1620 the English textile industry suffered a slump, forcing producers to change their lines and to search for new outlets; for northern France the 1630s began a decline (**152** ch. 6); for Hondschoote in Flanders the period 1640–45 saw the onset of a downward trend, but Leiden did not experience one until 1654.

Mining and metallurgy appear to have prospered in some areas of Europe during the Thirty Years War, but not in others. The famous Swedish *Kopparkompaniet*, founded in 1619 to exploit the general demand for copper, was only successful up to 1626, but the mines at Falun continued to prosper until the late 1650s. In Germany, figures for copper production in the seventeenth century do not show any clear trend, though it is known that copper mining had increased in the sixteenth century, especially in Bohemia. Figures for brass production partly help to fill the gap, since manufacture of brass was dependent on the supply of copper. The brass-making centres of Germany were in the Lower Rhine (around Aachen) and in Silesia and the Tyrol, and they gradually increased their output during the war years.

German silver production increased in the first half of the sixteenth century and then declined until 1618. The famous Marienberg mines in Saxony and those at Saigerhütten in Thuringia both reached their peaks before 1556. The total annual production of German silver fell from 360 tonnes in the 1540s to a low of 120 tonnes during the Thirty Years War, before recovering in the later seventeenth and early eighteenth centuries, though the Marienberg mines took longer to recover (**129** ch. 4).

Malleable iron was in great demand as the war progressed and Swedish production increased five-fold between 1600 and 1720. However, in France and Spain, iron production appears to have grown only slowly during the war years. Where fighting and troop movements interfered with local production, ironworks could suffer temporary loss of work or even closure. There was an increase in production of weapons at St Etienne during the wars, but this was offset by a decline in the number of ironworks in the Cévennes between 1540 and 1640 (**129** p. 79). In the late 1620s and early 1630s England shipped cast-iron cannon to the Dutch from her large foundries in the Weald.

In Germany iron production had increased during the sixteenth century and then declined during the seventeenth, though once again there was regional variation. Production in the Steirmark region increased from 10,000 tonnes in 1500 to 16,000 tonnes in 1750, but in the Upper Palatinate it declined markedly, especially during the war period (**152** ch. 7 p. 203).

Armaments industries such as those at Essen in Westphalia obviously prospered during the war years, and garrisoned towns generally were cushioned from the worst effects, as the experiences of Aachen and Minden indicate. There was an increase in demand for warships by the maritime powers during the war and this in turn strengthened demand for naval equipment. In many regions of Europe the war gave a boost to local industries such as rope-making, saw-milling, saltpetre and gunpowder. However, both in Germany and Europe generally, war brought dislocation and added risks for industrial activities, and heavy industries benefited more from peace (**129**).

Trade

International trade was very important for the Mediterranean, Atlantic and Baltic countries. Once again, however, the statistics do not allow clear conclusions to be drawn. H. and P. Chaunu describe a decline in the trade between Seville and Spanish America dating from 1608, and E. J. Hamilton's figures on the import of American silver indicate a depression throughout the seventeenth century up to 1660 (**86** p. 107). According to the Chaunus the general crisis of the early 1620s was due to the failure to finance a growing volume of trade. However, the link between the Seville trade and the Atlantic trade is not as clear-cut as the Chaunus thought. According to Posthumus, the reversal of trend in Dutch domestic prices came after 1650–60, which was some thirty years after the reversal at Seville. It could be argued that the Atlantic trade actually increased after 1620 since the Dutch and English were also involved in it. Certainly Brazilian sugar production doubled between 1620 and 1650 (**16** p. 13).

In the north of Europe, the Sound was an important filter for international trade. It represented almost all commercial connections between the Baltic and West Europe, and the Sound toll registers indicate a significant fall in the number of ships passing through it from 1619 – although there is no data regarding the tonnage or value of this trade. A. E. Christensen worked out a 'lastage' duty at Elsinore, where dues were paid, and concluded that in 1581–1620 there was a steady increase, followed after 1623 by a steady fall. These figures are open to criticism and Steensgaard argues that a 'turning point' can be located in 1639, though there were many fluctuations in the whole period 1620–50. Only after the late 1650s can a real depression be said to have set in (**87**, **147**).

The toll records suggest that the total carrying capacity of the German trade fleet fell during the Thirty Years War, but that was from a 'peak' as far back as 1570. German ships were increasingly used by Spain and Italy after 1621 as part of Spain's attempt to oust the Dutch from the Baltic. From 1607, there was a Spanish–Hanse agreement concerning the carrying of Dutch goods which even the truce did not disrupt. Shortage of corn in Italy after the 1580s opened up the prospect of a German–Mediterranean commercial link using Hamburg, Lübeck or Danzig. However, this only served to increase grain prices and freight charges. When the period of food shortage in Italy passed, the German trade diversified. Metals, shipbuilding materials, and linens were sent to Italy in return for wine, fruit, spices and oil. However, in general, the Thirty Years War put a break on the expansion of Germany's mercantile fleet, especially in comparison with her competitors (**152** ch. 7 p. 207).

Foreign trade was really a form of war. Most maritime governments followed a policy of protection in the belief that the total market for goods was limited and that expansion of production for any one country could only be achieved by breaking into markets normally served by another. Between 1620 and 1670 England and the Dutch succeeded in finding new markets for their goods or colonial re-exports, and since their existing markets in Germany, Poland and Spain contracted during this period, this meant increased commercial competition in the New World and the East. Spain in particular felt it necessary to protect her Imperial bases by waging economic warfare against the Dutch, especially after 1621.

It is possible to see Spain's struggle after the termination of the truce in 1621 as one for economic survival, faced as she was by intense pressure from the Dutch, rather than as a quest to establish hegemony in Europe (**111** and **112**). The concern shown by four Royal Councils in Madrid (those of War, State, Portugal and the Indies) about the deteriorating commercial position of Spain during the years of the truce (1609–21) led to the view that renewed hostilities would be better than the old terms of agreement. These terms had removed all obstacles to Dutch trade with Portugal and Spain; left Antwerp blockaded, to Amsterdam's advantage; allowed the Dutch to dominate the north–south carrying trade; increased Dutch trade in the Baltic at the expense of the Hanse towns; allowed the Dutch to expand in the East and West Indies; and given the Dutch opportunities to polarise attitudes in Europe towards Spain. To reverse these trends, Spain sought to impose economic embargoes against the Dutch and increase naval expenditure.

In 1621 Spain created new armadas in Flanders, Galicia and Gibraltar to add to her naval forces at Cadiz and Lisbon. Yet before 1639 they were used to protect Spain's commercial traffic and to disrupt that of the Dutch rather than to engage the enemy's navy. Only the armada of Flanders caused any real loss to the Dutch, but the armada at Gibraltar forced the Dutch to strengthen their convoys into the Mediterranean. Similarly the Flanders armada forced the Dutch to use convoys to protect their routes to the Sound, England and France. This, and the many losses that followed, forced up Dutch freight and insurance charges. It also threatened the Dutch North Sea fishing interests, especially after 1625, and was a constant problem to the South Holland fleets, right to the end of the war.

Commissioners of Commerce were appointed in Bilbao, Oporto, Lisbon, Seville, and San Lucar to tighten up on boarding regulations. Eventually the famous *Almirantazgo de los paises septentrionales* (inspectorate for commerce) was established in October 1624 to control the trade between northern Europe and Andalusia. It was a very efficient customs system based in Seville but operating in all Andalusian ports. Another *almirantazgo* was formed in Flanders and others in the Baltic, supported by new commercial courts. However, the contraction of those sectors of Spanish commerce where the Dutch had dominated before 1621 caused real hardship for many Spanish, Italian and Portuguese ports [**doc. 18**].

This economic warfare was extended to northern Europe when from 1625–29 Spain imposed a total river blockade, and then limited embargoes. The blockade was very effective, causing cheese and butter prices in Holland to fall markedly, along with those of wine and herring. However, where the blockade harmed Flemish commerce it was partially lifted in 1629, and it was weakened further when the Spaniards were driven from Wesel, Rheinberg, Lingen and Orsay between 1629 and 1634.

The changing pattern of Dutch trade that these measures enforced had a wider influence on European economic development between 1621 and 1648. In the 1620s the Hanseatic grain trade was given a boost, while the Dutch–Baltic trade slumped. When Sweden threatened the Habsburgs in north Europe, the Dutch–Baltic trade revived and, due to a series of poor harvests in Portugal and Spain, Bordeaux and other west-coast French ports acted as entrepôts for the Dutch carrying trade. However, only after 1640, when the Portuguese had rebelled against Spain, did the Dutch begin to deal directly once more with Iberian ports. The Dutch had also lost supplies of salt from Setubal and Valencia and this had to be replaced with salt from La Rochelle which was inferior in quality. Salt prices soared and this affected the prices of salt-related items.

Although Portuguese–Dutch trade revived after 1640, the embargoes and the Dunkirk fleet maintained economic pressure on the Dutch. Dutch colonial investments fell back and by 1641 the West India Company shares were beginning to decline in value. The Company lost political influence as a result. In 1645 the Dutch army was refused funds from Holland, where the 'peace party' had gained control. There was still strong resistance to the idea of peace from Friesland, Utrecht, and Zeeland, but the great commercial centres of Holland now wanted to promote European trade and this required peace.

Until 1627 Spain could argue with justification that her economic warfare had harmed Dutch trade and commerce. However, after 1635, and particularly after 1640 when Portugal and her overseas empire in Africa, America and Asia was opened to Dutch merchants, Spain realised that she could not win the economic battle and sought peace. By then the Dutch were in a position to impose their own terms and were more willing to accede.

Currencies, prices, wages

The period 1600–40 witnessed a steady contraction in the issue of money. This was true of France between 1608–35; of Milan in 1607–09 and especially 1619–22; of Lisbon in 1619–22; and of London in 1617–20 and 1627–36. Bullion remained important because it served to adjust trading balances and bolster a credit system that was heavily tied to coin transactions. Yet the records of the *Casa de Contratación* at Seville show that the high point of bullion shipments to Spain was reached in the 1590s, and that by the 1640s gold cargoes had fallen to two–fifths of that level. This took place when the need for a stable currency was increasing, and Spanish bullion found its way to Poland, Russia, the Levant, India, the East Indies and China.

Many financial partnerships were established to deal with Spain – for example, the Fuggers and Welsers in Germany and the Spinolas in Genoa. Yet as the import of gold and silver declined so money became 'tight'. This forced devaluations on various European governments. Copper *maravedis* (coins) in Spain had to be restamped at higher rates in 1603, 1636 and 1641. This led eventually to unstable monetary conditions, as copper coins took a larger share of the currencies. Also, since more silver than gold was imported between 1601 and 1660, the value of gold increased. All the exchanges of Venice, Paris, London and Amsterdam which had used gold currency as a fictitious base were adversely affected. The link between contracts and real money was threatened.

Many public banks were established to service the needs of governments. Venice had a Banco Giro (1619), and the Banco della Piazza di Rialto (at least up to 1633); Amsterdam had the famous Wisselbank from 1609 and there were banks in Rotterdam and Delft. They attempted to give the international system an element of stability since they were detached from the vagaries of local monetary systems. Even so, devaluations continued to occur all over Europe as the gap between supplies of bullion and the different local monetary systems widened after 1619–22.

Despite the general use of silver, it is still difficult to express the price of goods in common monetary terms. Most economic activity was localised and price levels varied. Spain and Italy had high silver prices, whereas Poland had much lower ones. War, high freight costs and a generally low level of capital investment combined to preserve these regional price variations. While farm prices remained high in most areas until the end of the Thirty Years War, despite cyclical fluctuations, industrial prices were much lower; this increased the search for extra-European markets and gave added tension to commercial rivalries. In the north of Europe there was some success in readjusting the old patterns, but in the Mediterranean the 1620s ushered in a period of decline and although in Spain and Italy prices rose again afterwards, the

Thirty Years War helped to pave the way for the shift in commercial hegemony to trade outlets in north-west Europe.

It might appear that, throughout Europe, the cost of living was very high in line with food prices. Certainly in Valencia the real wages of craftsmen in the building trade fell after 1600, as was the case in England (**110** p. 90). Yet, in Spain generally, wages and prices remained close together between 1500 and 1650, so that wages more or less kept up with inflation. In the Low Countries it appears that wage rates remained stable after 1590 although it is difficult to be sure. In Italy it seems that wages were increasing throughout the seventeenth century (**152** ch. 1). However, increased wage rates meant increased production costs and these brought extra difficulties to local economies. In general the war unbalanced the European economy and although some areas temporarily profited, only after 1648 could more stable patterns of integration emerge.

As for Germany, the large number of currencies, and the three different monetary areas of the thaler, gulden and mark, make generalisations about prices and wages very difficult. Even so it is possible to say that the war appears to have been only moderately inflationary, with food prices (especially for rye) rising up to 1640 but thereafter falling. Meat prices were often kept down by the action of farmers sheltering their cattle in towns when troops approached. There was a rise in real wages from about 1620 and the wage earner was not necessarily in a bad position during the war.

However, the inflation occasioned by the cheating money-changers – generally referred to as Kipper and Wipper – and the mushrooming of mints, had a damaging effect. Producers tended to refrain from taking their goods to market and trade was seriously threatened. There were disturbances in Bayreuth in 1621, and Halle and Magdeburg in 1622. By 1623 Alsace, Austria and Württemberg had legislated to fix the value of the mark at nine Reichstaler (13½ florins), which meant a devaluation of 25 per cent. Attempts were made to fix commodity prices which often led to a fall in the standard of living of many 'prosperous' bourgeois.

In Bavaria and other states, outgoings regularly exceeded income, and this was exacerbated in some areas by the effects of war. Nuremberg's public spending had been rising before the seventeenth century, but financial crises attendant upon the military activities of the years 1621–22, 1629–34 and 1646–48 stand out. Even so, financial institutions developed and expanded.

The Viatis and Peller trading and marketing partnership extended into money-lending and helped to establish the Nuremberg Exchange Bank in 1621. The Hamburg Bank, as it gained a reputation for honesty, allowed merchant bankers to transact exchange business on a larger scale and helped to establish the city as the wealthiest in Germany by 1648.

Public finance: Sweden, Spain, France

'The early modern state was, to a large extent, a military institution. Around half of its income in every year was spent on war, preparation for or liquidating the consequences of war' (**132** p. 14). Yet methods of financing war varied. Sweden was at war continually between 1600 and 1660 and the need to finance continental campaigns forced the government to establish a war economy based more on money and natural resources than goods. Rarely were Sweden's ordinary revenues – which in the 1620s amounted to 1.5 million silver thalers (see Note, p.vi) – sufficient [**doc. 19**]. The revenues of the crown were sold or pawned to raise lump sums in cash and by the middle of the seventeenth century almost three–fifths of the 'ordinary revenue' (ancient taxes on land) was in private hands. Although this was fraught with danger for the future and led to the unpopular *reduktion* in the 1650s, for the crucial years of expansion up to mid-century, Sweden could avoid the financial difficulties that faced other countries. There was no sale of honours; no major debasement of the coinage; and no minting of extra money. Sweden's debt remained quite modest until the reign of Charles XI, and only then did the government face bankruptcy.

In wartime 'extraordinary revenues' – such as the poll tax assessed *per capita* on practically the whole labouring population between the ages fifteen and sixty – were nearly always granted (**71** p. 79). Sweden could also depend on her excellent natural resources of copper and iron, the demand for which allowed her to avoid the worst effects of the monetary crises elsewhere. Control of the Prussian ship tolls, subsidies from France, and the military policy of 'living off the land' in Germany all made Sweden's war efforts pay for themselves. It was 'war by proxy' (**194**) and as long as war lasted this policy was successful. War finance was sufficient as long as the armies were victorious. Defeat threatened the whole structure, however, and peace would destroy it.

Spain faced her financial difficulties in a different way. Olivares' government managed to solve most of its problems, but always in an atmosphere of tension and always at great cost. The war with the Dutch was renewed in the full knowledge that bullion imports from the New World had fallen. The greater part of the revenue had to be raised from the taxpayers of Castile. From 1610 to 1628 the annual royal budget increased from 12 million to more than 15 million ducats. About half of this went immediately to service the royal debt. Until 1621 military spending took a further one–third of the budget (about 4 or 5 million ducats), but afterwards the demands of war forced the government to borrow more. Between 1615 and 1625 expenditure increased by 150 per cent as against a 25 per cent increase in revenue (**201** p. 65).

However, the bankruptcy of 1627 and the effects of the Dutch action at Matanzas in 1628 seriously reduced the crown's capacity to raise credit. The minting of *vellon* (copper coins) did serious damage to the rate of exchange and had the paradoxical effect of boosting Swedish copper exports due to the consequent demand for extra copper. However, at least it allowed the government to raise 2.6 million ducats in 1621–26. When the minting of *vellon* waned it was replaced by a sales tax (the *millones*). As the Thirty Years War dragged on, Philip IV was forced to reduce his own personal budget and to alienate royal estates and mortgage many other sources of revenue to raise money for the war. Many of these methods undermined the traditional basis of the crown's financial structure and also the stability of the government.

Increasingly Spain's satellites were called upon to contribute money and men for the war effort by way of *asientos* (government contracts) and extraordinary 'war taxes'. Milan, Naples, and Sicily were dragged into the Spanish financial maelstrom. As Stradling puts it, 'the Old World was called in to redress the balance of the New' (**201** p. 66). This is not to belittle the continued importance of bullion imports. Although the amounts imported never represented more than a fraction of the funds raised by the treasury, they continued to have value as security for loans, and even after 1627 bankers were prepared to help finance Spain's war-efforts.

The 'Union of Arms' had actually been accepted in principle in Spain from 1627, but the military setbacks in Flanders and Italy (1629–33) involved such loss of life and money that the Council of War was forced to increase its demands for new recruits on an already discouraged Castilian nobility as well as on Milan and Naples. The Pope allowed Spain to levy extra ecclesiastical taxation, and copper coins were again minted. After the Mantuan

61

war Philip IV was advised that he could rely on 7 million ducats annually for six years, and it was on this assumption that he rejected the current Dutch peace proposals. Yet war with France forced Philip to fight on two fronts and use resources that should have gone to Flanders.

In 1647 Spain was bankrupt again, at a time when she was committed to the provision of 13 million ducats for her various armies. A financial decree of 1647 managed to get Madrid over the worst of the crisis and allowed Philip IV to carry on the war with France. Thus Spain continued to finance her commitments in the Thirty Years War, even though, paradoxically, her economic infrastructure was never in a healthy condition.

Since it is common to regard the Thirty Years War as the 'making of France', it is surprising to discover how precarious her financial position was in the years up to 1648. Richelieu had never been secure at court and Marie de Medici constantly encouraged Louis XIII to dismiss the Cardinal. However, with the 'Day of Dupes' in November 1630 the King reasserted himself against his mother and her supporters and gave Richelieu the opportunity to commit France to a more belligerent foreign policy. Yet France was unprepared for a long-term series of campaigns in Europe, and war was not officially declared until 1635 in order to give Richelieu more time to build up his resources. The Mantuan campaign had revealed many weaknessess in French military organisation and financial commitments had been entered into with the Dutch (1630) and the Swedes (1631) which France could ill afford.

When war was declared, Claude Bullion, the Financial Minister, attempted to protect the flow of cash by devaluing the *livre tournois* (money of account) in March 1636 and by issuing more coins (28 million livres were issued in 1625–59 with the first great burst coming in 1640–44). Without these measures it is doubtful whether France would have been able to continue fighting as long as she did (**81**). Under Henry IV about 8 per cent of the total revenue had come from the sale of offices; in the 1620s the proportion had risen to 30 per cent and by the late 1630s it was 50 per cent and the market was almost saturated. Also, although the office-holders continued to pay the *Paulette* (an annual tax which allowed holders to retain their offices as if they were pieces of property to be bequeathed or transferred as they saw fit), they increasingly resented the way the crown treated them as milch cows. Thus Bullion's measures were a much-needed stimulant to exports, an encouragement to private investment in royal financial transactions, and they helped to reduce the costs of cash subsidies to France's allies.

As expected, military expenditure increased after the declaration of war. It had averaged less than 16 million livres (see Note, p.vi) a year in the 1620s, but after 1635 it rose to over 33 million, and by 1640 had reached 38 million. Military expenditure could account for between 60 per cent and 75 per cent of the total of the current account (**14** graph 5). Borrowing also increased, so that by 1640 the total indebtedness of the French crown was 38 million livres.

Many 'extraordinary taxes' were devised and 40 million livres each year came from new tax contracts (*traites*). Both direct and indirect taxes were increased and from 1637 there was a new military tax (*subsistances*) to tide the army over the winter months. The indirect taxes were very difficult to collect. Rural poverty, the lack of coins in circulation prior to 1640–44, the effect of famine, plague and the presence of troops had all reduced the likelihood that these taxes would be paid in full.

Figures for indirect taxation are very misleading. Not all the projected increase would have been expected to reach the treasury because local collectors always subtracted their 'expenses', and tax farmers always misrepresented the totals collected. Towns levied their own local taxes, the sheer number of which could cause confusion. Indeed, by 1641 the revenue from the *aides* (levied mostly on drink) had practically come to a standstill. Thus revenues from both direct taxes (principally the *taille*) and indirect ones were never as high as the treasury would have liked, and some of the tactics that Bullion used to ensure more efficiency in collection alienated many of the office-holders, who mistrusted his intentions.

Bullion died in December 1640, leaving Bouthillier as sole Finance Minister. He immediately increased the government's borrowing. However, arrears in the *taille* eventually forced him to call for reduced government spending, for fear that falling confidence in the government's financial probity would result in military defeat. France began to fear bankruptcy. Even the French victory at Rocroi in May 1643 could not dispel the fear that government spending was over-reaching itself. A dispute over war estimates had already led to the dismissal of the War Minister, Sublet des Noyers, in April.

When Mazarin became Chief Minister in 1643 he replaced Bouthillier, but government spending steadily increased. Royal borrowing also grew, to ensure that the various French armies had a continuous flow of cash. Yet there had been little improvement in the revenue-raising system and the office-holders were in no position to increase their payments. In fact direct taxes were reduced during 1643–47, though an attempt by the treasury to register new proposals for raising money with the *Parlement* of Paris brought widespread opposition in 1645 and 1648 which delayed the peace negotiations at Westphalia. Mazarin had hoped that Spain's financial position would crack under the heavy pressures of the war, but by 1647 France was herself bankrupt (though bankruptcy was not declared until 1648). Thus, just as peace came to Europe, political temperatures in France were rising over government financial policy. Spain felt emboldened to continue her war with France, sensing that widespread dissatisfaction in the French provinces would increase her chances of victory enormously.

Revolt and reaction: Europe in crisis?

Conditions such as subsistence crises, periodic harvest failures and excesses of public financial policies were intermittent, short-term adversities. They gave rise to numerous forms of collective violence, ranging from sporadic tax and food riots, to agrarian and urban revolts, to rebellious movements by inferior social groups as part of much bigger revolutionary disorders. These short-term economic factors had their greatest effect upon the unprivileged – urban workers, poor peasants and rural labourers – rather than those higher up the social scale.

France was the classic state where the government's exactions and poor harvests played major roles in fomenting localised disturbances, especially in the south-west and in Normandy (**161**). In Provence, for example, there were 374 revolts in 119 years (1596–1715), and in the period 1625–75 they were usually directed against the demands of the state. In the *généralité* of Bordeaux, the *taille* had remained constant from 1610 to 1632 at about 1 million livres, but in 1635 it was increased to 2 million, in 1644 to 3 million and in 1648 to 4 million. The violent reaction, known as the *Ormée* of Bordeaux, lasted from 1651 to 1653 when the city was starved into submission by a royal army.

However, apart from these rural and urban riots and disturbances, there were other forms of revolt in early modern Europe. First there were conspiracies and *coups d'état* – which were mainly limited to the aristocratic section of the population. Then there were provincial, regional and separatist rebellions such as the *Nu-*

pieds revolt in Normandy in 1639 and the revolts in Aragon, Catalonia and Portugal. Finally, there were kingdom-wide civil wars against monarchies involving the entire society and based on noble and aristocratic leadership. Zagorin has suggested that 'it seems to have been the case in early modern Europe that the wider the social participation in a revolution, the smaller, as a rule, the importance of short-run...phenomena in giving rise to it' (**153** Vol. I p. 127). This is not to suggest that peasants and lesser urban people were insusceptible to the influence of political ideas, values and ideologies – as the role of political goals in the German peasant war of the sixteenth century indicates. Rather, in most localised disturbances where the elites were not involved, the violence was usually aimed at those most obviously identifiable as the cause of economic hardship or fiscal exploitation: seldom the landlord but mainly royal tax agents or hoarders and sellers of grain and consumables. Only occasionally were these immediate grievances subsumed within a wider vision of change and reform.

It is difficult, though, to treat these short-term economic circumstances in isolation because they intersected with other conditions as well as with expectations, beliefs and perceptions. Economic forces operated in a complex manner and their political significance depended on the way they mixed with religious and social discontents in each case.

Some historians argue that longer-term economic movements had a cumulative impact on the position of entire social groups, occupations and orders – as in the period after 1610–20 when the economic climate changed from expansion to contraction. In these circumstances, it is argued, aristocracies and élites could be drawn into political revolt. Yet the reasons for the reversal of the secular trend, as well as its extent, are matters of debate, and the incidence and timing of the downturn varied within the European economy. Some historians have represented the conditions prevailing after 1620 as a pervasive crisis of both the European economies and societies – the alleged 'general crisis of the seventeenth century'. This has been used to explain the disparate developments of the time including the Thirty Years War and the series of contemporaneous revolts that occurred in mid-century. This crisis has been viewed as at once social, political and economic.

However, other historians dislike speaking of a 'crisis' whose chronology not only remains vague but is held to have lasted up to fifty years and longer. As Steensgaard has pointed out: 'the seventeenth-century crisis was not a universal retrogression, but it hit the various sectors at different times and to a different extent...it is impossible to pin-point a time or period when European trade and industry as a whole was hit by a depression' (**147** p. 40). With these doubts, the thesis of a general crisis which is pictured as an interlocking economic, social and political phenomenon, and which provided the origin and explanation of the revolutions and wars of the mid-seventeenth century, must be even more improbable. As Rabb indicates: 'the progression of events in economic and demographic history cannot be made to conform to the stages that have been perceived in other aspects of seventeenth-century developments.... And the important changes that did take place do not fit convincingly into any of the broader frameworks of "crisis" that have been imposed on the period' (**36** p. 90).

Most of the proponents of the general crisis theory merely offer a circular argument that the revolts of mid-century prove the existence of an antecedent crisis. Yet, as Zagorin notes, this crisis 'needs to be demonstrated independently of its supposed consequences before we can begin to consider whether there was a connection between the two' (**153** Vol. I p. 138). Historians have not succeeded in doing this as yet.

On the other hand, as Zagorin again suggests, 'it might be easier to accept the general crisis if the revolutions of the time all really did conform to a common model. But they failed to do so...they belong instead to several different types' (**153** vol. I pp. 138–39). Stone, for instance, draws on a variety of theories of revolution in order to identify and explain the preconditions of the English Civil War. However, for supporters of the thesis of the general crisis and contemporaneous revolutions, his conclusion is not very helpful: 'to explain in a coherent way why things happened the way they did has necessitated the construction of multiple helix chains of causation more complicated than those of DNA itself. The processes of society are more complex than those of nature' (**148** p. 146). The implication is that although it may be possible to take a dispassionate look at individual rebellions, revolts and civil wars and apply a particular definition of revolution to them, it is much more difficult to use any single definition to cover a whole variety of events, processes and structures in different parts of Europe.

Most of the definitions referred to by Stone were written by modern social scientists whose frames of reference were developments in eighteenth-century Europe (eg **113**). When applied to the numerous types of disturbances in sixteenth and seventeenth century Europe, they appear both too wide and too narrow. Zagorin, hoping to avoid this objection, has defined the concept of revolution as 'any attempt by subordinate groups through the use of violence to bring about (1) a change of government or its policy, (2) a change of regime, or (3) a change of society, whether this attempt is justified by reference to past conditions or to an as yet unattained future ideal' (**153** vol. I p. 17). Yet this definition still blurs the distinction between rebellion and revolution and it rules out the idea of counter-revolution as being a revolutionary phenomenon since the governments which initiate it cannot be categorised as 'subordinate groups'. The first rebellion in European history that became known to contemporaries as a revolution – where the word was used in a political sense – was the English revolution of 1688; yet the concept still retained elements of its traditional meaning of circular motion – as a *restoration* of a legal order that James II had violated.

It is true that measures and demands for the restoration or maintenance of a system can unintentionally give rise to innovations and changes, but this does not mean the historian has to accept 'revolution' as the generic class containing all revolutionary occurrences of whatever kind. Despite the work of social scientists, there is still no adequate typology or classification of revolutions.

Although social tensions did exist in many European states, the ordering of society in early modern Europe was generally unfavourable for the type of class solidarity that most of the modern concepts of revolution require. As Elliott points out: 'A society grouped into corporations, divided into orders and linked vertically by powerful ties of kinship and clientage cannot be expected to behave in the same way as a society divided into classes' (**99** p. 117). Kamen shows how the leaders of the people never ceased to question the activities of central government, but that the common cry 'ancient rights', though productive of some genuinely radical acts and revolutionary terminology in the modern sense, was essentially non-revolutionary in most instances (**116** chs. 9 and 10). Even in the few cases of kingdom-wide civil war, the rebels were mostly motivated by the desire to defend the *status quo* against innovatory central governments, despite the fact that they were often driven by the pace of events to formulate theories of resistance which went beyond the traditionally accepted limits.

Some historians argue that the political, administrative and social structures of European states were under strain from the pressures of war and that these tensions initiated a 'crisis of government' which then led to the major rebellions in France, England, Spain and elsewhere (**70**, **133**). The difficulty about this thesis is that there is no definitive way of either disproving or proving it. Nor is it clear that the main states of Europe were closer to breakdown in the 1640s than they had been in the 1560s (**99**), or were to be in the 1680s (**124**). Even if it could be shown that they were, it is clear that the reasons would not be the same in each case.

However, as this book has suggested, the Thirty Years War certainly influenced policy decisions in all European nations, and there must be a link between the years of comprehensive warfare in central Europe after 1620 and the heightening of tensions both within and between states. To accommodate and sustain wartime developments there had to be an increase in state bureaucracy, state finance and state intervention in the economy and society. Government policy was indeed a great motivator of change and reaction.

By the late 1630s and early 1640s, however, it was beyond the power of any one state to terminate the fighting. The juggernaut of war had developed its own momentum. Once raised, armies seemed to be laws unto themselves and the activities of the commanders on the spot often enfeebled peace negotiations and kept local populations aggressive. Governments were fastened into a situation they could do little to control. As the costs of war grew, they felt less inclined to settle without making clear-cut gains. The more desperate the situation became, the more desperate were the attempts made to secure a favourable negotiating position.

Thus the Thirty Years War itself created a sense of accelerating disaster and provided a context for revolt and rebellion. If a crisis is defined as the stage directly antecedent to relaxation, then, as Rabb has pointed out, 'the disillusionment with violence and confrontation was the first of the changes that eventually led Europeans to stop struggling with the consequences of the events of the early sixteenth century' so that only with peace could aggressions subside, new structures become feasible and a 'resolution' occur (**36** p. 145). The Thirty Years War should not, therefore, be seen merely as a consequence of a deeper malaise in Europe. It had a more positive role in creating and heightening many of the tensions that the historians of the mid-seventeenth-century crisis ascribe to other factors.

6   Religion and Diplomacy

The Thirty Years War presented most European rulers with the necessity of making judgements that balanced the interests of religion with those of politics and economics. An examination of the confusing pattern of allegiances during the war indicates that although religious disagreement was an important element in almost every political crisis, the confessional divisions were not clear-cut.

Pope Urban VIII and Cardinals Richelieu and Mazarin were all opposed, in their various ways, to Catholic Spain and the Catholic Emperor. The Elector of Saxony, a Lutheran, and the Elector of Bavaria, a Catholic, were hostile to Lutheran Sweden and Catholic Spain. Hesse–Cassel, a Calvinist state, often proved a reliable ally of Sweden and, along with Bavaria, was frequently pro-French. The conflicts in the Baltic ranged Sweden not just against Catholic Poland, but also Orthodox Russia and fellow-Lutheran Denmark. Gustavus Adolphus was a staunch Protestant, but once in Germany he readily accepted aid from France. Maximilian of Bavaria extended his territories with the agreement of Lutheran Saxony and Catholic France, but at the expense of the Emperor, Lutheran cities and the Calvinist Elector Palatine. Both Catholic and Protestant delegates at the Westphalian negotiations were open to French subsidies, and at Münster the Bishops of Würzburg and Bamberg were quick to abandon the Catholic interest. The suppression of Protestantism by Ferdinand II in Austria and Bohemia, and by Richelieu in France, was based on a mix of political and religious reasons: Protestants, it was claimed, not only threatened spiritual unity but opposed royal absolutism and were covert republicans (**40** pp. 96–99).

The contest of Emperor and Princes in Germany was not just to decide the religious complexion of the Empire, but whether the Emperor was to be head of a unified monarchy or a titular president of a federation. In this light, the Edict of Restitution of 1629, regarded by the Emperor as a means of imposing religious uniformity, was seen by the Princes as a way of establishing

Habsburg imperialism at their expense, and provoked opposition from the Electors. This dual nature of the contest was evident again in 1648 when the protest of Pope Innocent X against the Westphalian compromise with the Protestants [**doc. 9**], led the negotiators to draw up a special 'anti-protest' clause, signed by all parties, condemning Innocent's attitude.

However, it would be wrong to assume that, because of these paradoxes and contradictions, the political leaders were not much influenced by their faiths. While it is true that Wallenstein's religious convictions defy definition (**69**) and were justly mistrusted by both Protestants and Catholics, other leaders sincerely believed in the exclusive claims of their respective churches. Ferdinand II, Maximilian of Bavaria, Tilly and Richelieu were devout Catholics; Gustavus Adolphus, the Electors of Brandenburg, Saxony, and the Palatinate and Bernard of Weimar were equally unswerving Protestants. Yet most leaders were not prepared to let spiritual concerns dominate secular matters, and 'reasons of state' often proved far more compelling than the laws of God as a guide to political decision-making. This was as much the case with Ferdinand II, Richelieu, the German Princes and Gustavus Adolphus, as it was with the 'Most Catholic Kings' of Spain.

Ferdinand II and Lamormaini

There is no doubting Ferdinand II's devotion to his church. As Lamormaini, his Jesuit confessor and adviser, was at pains to point out, the Emperor had an elaborate ritual to go through on waking each morning which included meditations and two masses as well as kissing the floor five times in memory of Christ's five wounds (**100** p. 72). In his *Virtutes Fernandi II*, Lamormaini published all the stories about the Emperor's hatred of Protestant sins and delight in Catholic conversions and laid the foundations of the dynastic political myth of the *Pietas Austriaca* – a confessional re-interpretation of traditional ideas of wise government in terms of seventeenth-century absolutism.

Ferdinand seemed to match up to this glowing picture. He was a man for getting things done and on the face of it his imperial policy was shaped by his religious programme, for which Lamormaini was largely responsible. Until 1630 Ferdinand pressed for the persecution of Protestants within the *Erblande*, resisted any compromise with them in Germany, and demanded the full implementation of the Edict of Restitution. Both the Emperor and Lamormaini thought the requirements of the Catholic faith should be paramount in policy-making. Ferdinand was assured by his Jesuit adviser that the victories over the Bohemians, the Palatinate and Denmark in the 1620s were all part of a divine mission to restore Catholicism in the Empire.

However, despite recent attempts at interpreting Lamormaini's correspondence with Ferdinand, it is still difficult to assess what passed between them (**159, 160**). Lamormaini often reduced the political complexities of the European situation to simple spiritual formulas which provided inadequate guidance in the rough-and-tumble of diplomacy. He never understood Wallenstein's view of the German question and seemed unable to grasp that the tactics and policies of the Spanish Habsburgs were as much a product of reasons of state as missionary zeal. Spain in turn mistrusted Lamormaini's earlier opposition to the Emperor's intervention in Italy over the Mantuan succession and his naïve hope for an agreement between Paris and Vienna. The Edict of Restitution was seriously criticised in the electoral convention at Regensburg in 1630 and Ferdinand gradually recognised the need to balance the 'ideological' element of Catholic reform with other interests and ambitions. After 1630, while the Emperor continually consulted Lamormaini on the moral and religious aspects of his policy, in practice he often made his decisions in the framework of a traditional rationale of Habsburg imperialism.

There had been a history of Habsburg resistance to the influence of Papal nuncios and Papal wishes, especially over presentation to bishoprics, and in the sixteenth century 'Court Christians' – in the Emperor's Aulic Council – were more alive to 'reasons of state' than to the demands of the Council of Trent and the Inquisition. Despite Ferdinand II's initial drive to extend the Catholic Reformation in the Empire in the 1620s, the different interpretations of the Catholic 'mission' held by the various Catholic leaders, and the complexities of the European situation in wartime, forced Ferdinand back into a more familiar Habsburg mould.

Ferdinand's initial enthusiasm, encouraged by his successes in Styria, led him to equate Protestantism with disloyalty – an attitude that led logically to the Edict of Restitution. Yet his fervour was gradually compromised by the internal disputes of the Empire and the pressures of war. The proposition that 'all Catholics are loyal' did not bear examination. In this light, the meeting at Regensburg in 1630 must have been a great disappointment for Ferdinand. He had started the negotiations from a position of relative strength, but was manoeuvred into dismissing Wallenstein. He also failed to get a hearing for the idea of electing his son King of the Romans, or to win the approval of the Electors for aid for the Spanish cause in north Italy and the Netherlands. Nor could he prevent Maximilian of Bavaria continuing his talks with the French concerning a defensive alliance in the Empire. Admittedly he preserved a semblance of Catholic unity over the issue of the Edict, yet this was not to last long.

In the period between Regensburg and the peace of Prague, Wallenstein was re-called (and then assassinated); Gustavus Adolphus threatened Ferdinand's hereditary lands; Saxon troops marched into Bohemia; Lamormaini was increasingly involved in rancorous disputes with fellow Jesuits and older orders; and the Pope openly criticised Ferdinand's Italian policy. Although the battle of Nördlingen helped the Emperor to impose a Habsburg-dominated peace on Europe in 1635, it was not a peace that he would have settled for even as late as 1630, especially since it included withdrawal of the Edict of Restitution.

When Ferdinand II died in 1637, his son was faced with a deteriorating situation. Spain was involved in open war with France; Swedish power was still a threat in the north; Maximilian of Bavaria and the Catholic ecclesiastical Electors could not be fully trusted; the imperial armies now lacked solid military leadership; and the burdens of taxation and recruitment kept the internal situation in the hereditary lands unsettled. In addition to these problems, Bohemia and Moravia were continually the prey of foreign troops up to 1648 (the Swedes had their headquarters at Olomouc in the 1640s), and there was renewed war in Transylvania (1643–45). The Westphalian agreements revealed how far the Habsburg dynasty had lost its pre-eminence in the Empire. Despite their efforts, Ferdinand III and Trautmansdorf could not break down the growing gulf between 'Kaiser' and 'Reich' (**181, 172**).

However, as far as the *Erblande* was concerned, the peace of Westphalia allowed Ferdinand III untramelled sovereignty and, with limited exceptions in Silesia, Lower Austria and Hungary, the Emperor was free to press on with Catholic reform. The Pope's antagonism towards the peace sprang from the fact that his own secular influence had waned markedly despite the Edict of Restitution. Spain, France and England had already gained their various national churches, and confirmation of the principle of *cuis regio, eius religio*, together with the establishment of the base-date of 1624 for settling ecclesiastical accessions in central Europe, was yet further indication that the role of the Papacy (and hence of religion) in politics had been significantly weakened.

Richelieu, Maximilian and Gustavus Adolphus

For Richelieu, the problems of Italy and Germany were enmeshed. The diplomatic manoeuvring that preceded the meeting of the electoral college at Regensburg indicates how far Richelieu and his advisers were prepared to go to keep Habsburg troops out of Italy and Germany divided [**doc. 20**]. The French hoped that the Electors would force Ferdinand to dismiss Wallenstein and obstruct Lamormaini's 'Spanish' influence so that the Emperor would be encouraged to make peace in Italy.

The aim of this diplomatic mission was to show the German Princes that Richelieu was not interested in a war of religion, only in the preservation of 'German Liberties' and a common front against Spain and Habsburg absolutism. Accordingly, Maximilian of Bavaria was seen by the French as a counter-weight to Ferdinand's power, especially when the dismissal of Wallenstein left Tilly and the Catholic League's forces as the Emperor's main army. However, Ferdinand's concessions at Regensburg actually forestalled the French plan of creating a 'third force' around Maximilian and showed that many Catholic princes were not too enthusiastic about trading an Austrian for a French protectorate.

It was in Ferdinand's interests to keep France's Italian and German policies out of line. Thus the treaty of Regensburg with the French over the Mantuan war tied Louis XIII to renouncing his Protestant allies in Germany and to terminating any negotiations with Gustavus Adolphus. However, the treaty was never ratified by the French government and the Italian war was not settled until 1631 and the peace of Cherasco. Hence, Richelieu continued to explore the possibilities of a Bavarian defensive alliance and a French-subsidised Swedish invasion.

Richelieu was at pains to point out to Maximilian that, since the issues at hand were not religious, there was little to fear from yet another Protestant invasion. Yet Gustavus invaded Germany before any compact had been reached between France and Bavaria, and this confirmed Maximilian's suspicions that the French were in no real position to control a Swedish advance or prevent Swedish Protestantism from enveloping the Empire (**155, 156**). He never liked the French reliance on Sweden and thought Richelieu had misinterpreted Gustavus Adolphus' aims. Yet he was also aware that if France abandoned her interest in Bavaria as a 'third force' and turned instead to the Netherlands or England, then his territories and titles would be in danger on three fronts (**31**).

More immediate than this, for Maximilian, was the threat posed by the Spanish in the Lower Palatinate. Indeed, it was the spectre of a Spanish take-over in the Palatinate and the invasion of Gustavus Adolphus which finally propelled him into a Franco–Bavarian defensive alliance in 1631. Thus Maximilian tried to protect himself from Swedish and Spanish intervention on the one hand, yet attempted to preserve his rights and obligations as an Elector and Prince of the Empire on the other. This required him to treat with both France and the Emperor, and at times this act on the diplomatic tightrope came close to disaster.

The treaty of Bärwalde placed Richelieu in an embarrassing position. The negotiations had been completed quickly so that Richelieu could claim some control over Sweden's activities in Germany [**doc 5, 20**]. However, many ambiguities remained and Richelieu was never sure if Gustavus fully understood the French view of the invasion, or what Swedish ambitions were.

From the outbreak of the Thirty Years War, Gustavus Adolphus had feared that the spread of Catholicism in central Europe might threaten not only the interests of Protestantism in Germany, but also Sweden's interests in the Baltic area. As early as 1620 he had suggested to the anti-Habsburg powers that Sweden should head a re-invigorated Protestant League in the Empire. At the time, Christian IV of Denmark had upstaged the Swedes by offering to lead a broader Protestant alliance – which included England and the Netherlands – but it was clear that even before the formation of the Hague Coalition, Sweden already had plans for some form of intervention in Germany.

When Christian IV finally invaded Germany, he had it in mind to control the important bishoprics in the north, and gain control of trade along the Weser and Elbe. The control of cathedral chapters by Protestants had been a method of circumventing the Ecclesiastical Reservation of 1555, for by gaining a majority in the chapters, Protestants could ensure the election of Protestant Bishops. The administration of dioceses was a lucrative business and many Bishops sought to make their appointments hereditary. The rapidity of the Danish collapse left the Protestant cause in north Germany without a military protector. Despite continued doubts about Swedish intervention, the anti-Habsburg movement was content enough in 1630 to rely on the armed intervention of

Gustavus Adolphus. Indeed, Gustavus would have exploited the religious aspects of his invasion had not the Swedish government felt it prudent to play down the visions of a Protestant crusade in case potential Catholic sympathisers were alienated.

It should have come as no surprise that Gustavus Adolphus, once established in Germany, outlined a project for a league of Protestant Princes under his direction (*Norma Futurarum Actionum*). Though Oxenstierna later claimed that the King had merely 'intended to safeguard his kingdom and the Baltic Sea, and to liberate the oppressed lands, and thereafter to proceed as things might fall out [and that] to begin with he had not intended to go as far as he did' (**193** p. 156), the end product was always likely to be a form of security system similar to his previous designs. Gustavus did not seriously consider claiming the Imperial throne (**193** p. 164), since this might have deprived him of French support and would certainly have affronted John George of Saxony. As Richelieu pointed out to Gustavus, there would have been little point in dividing central Europe once more into two powerful factions based on religious antagonism, since such a state of affairs would have benefited the King of Spain far more than either Louis XIII or Gustavus [**doc. 20**].

Yet, while he lived, the Swedish King retained the desire for a total victory over both branches of the Habsburg family. He offered Germany a military dictatorship which would have paid only lip-service to princely 'Liberties'. Fortunately the battle of Lützen was a reminder to all that the Thirty Years War was not, by its very nature, a war to be won by a final campaign or a great victory.

Spain

By the seventeenth century the Spanish 'system' had, almost everywhere, given rise to that conglomeration of fear, admiration and local rumour known as the 'Black Legend' (**185, 189**). In terms of policy-making, Philip II had fused spiritual and secular considerations so that the Spanish 'mission' was seen as the maintenance of the Catholic Commonwealth, which in turn justified the domino-theory of territorial strategy and the deployment of Spanish troops. To many Europeans, the bureaucrats, soldiers and emissaries of the Catholic Kings seemed bloated with the self-righteousness, superiority and arrogance which fed the legend.

In France Spanish envoys worked tirelessly to uphold Spain's influence and deepen the distrust shown to the Bourbon dynasty.

They often sought to widen the gulf between the Huguenots and royal authority. They hoped that the same intertwining of magnate factionalism and Protestant dissent that had given rise to the French wars of Religion in the sixteenth century could be rekindled in the seventeenth to prevent France from entering the European war against Spain. Richelieu, though a Cardinal and a devout Catholic, was shrewd enough to realise that a policy of divorcing religious from political dissent, both at home and abroad, was the most suitable one for preserving France's interests and for weakening Spanish influence. He thus guaranteed the Huguenots freedom of conscience and limited freedom of worship in France, while he attacked Spain in the Valtelline. As he explained, 'it cannot be doubted that the Spaniards aspire to universal domination' (**201** p. 80).

In the United Provinces William of Orange's 'Apologia' of 1583, that celebrated piece of rebel propaganda against Philip II (**189** ch. 12), also stressed that Spain's main aim was world domination. The Palatinate took this theme up when it was threatened by Spanish intervention and joined with the United Provinces in being a hot-house for anti-Habsburg activities.

Yet in the Netherlands, as elsewhere, religion and the language of politics were inextricably entangled. There was a dispute between two extremes of the same Calvinist faith. The hard-line Calvinists, who were religiously intolerant, supported a strong central government under the House of Orange. To them, the moderates, who were associated with Oldenbarneveldt and stood for provincial 'Liberties' and the rule of the merchant oligarchs (the 'Regents'), were pro-Spanish and anti-Orange. When Oldenbarneveldt was executed in 1618 the decentralised republicanism that he stood for was replaced by the semi-monarchic rule of the Stadtholders Maurice and Frederick Henry, though the squabbles over religion continued to colour the political and economic disputes within the United Provinces throughout the Thirty Years War. This mix of religious, economic and political tensions gave Spain constant hope that a favourable peace might be arranged in the period when the rule of the Stadtholders proved unpopular.

If Spain had been on the defensive in the years leading up to 1618, she was certainly on the offensive in the 1620s. Feria's occupation of the Valtelline; Bedmar's support for the occupation of the Rhineland states in the same year; Olivares' Baltic designs; Spanish help for the Huguenots; and Philip III's alliance with Persia were all signs that Madrid was prepared to press Spain's interests more forcefully after 1618. Thus it seemed to Richelieu that 'You Spaniards always have God and the Holy Virgin on your lips and a rosary in your hands, but you never do anything except for worldly ends' (**201** p. 106) [**doc. 20**]. Even the Popes, from Clement VIII onwards, warned Madrid that Spanish dominance in Italy and elsewhere was not a good thing either for the Papacy or the peace of Europe.

However, long before 1628, there had been a fear in some Spanish circles that Spain was over-extending herself and that another truce with the Dutch was preferable to a war with France and the possibility of total collapse. After the Swedish intervention a truce seemed even more urgent, and the government in Brussels was encouraged by Madrid to press forward with negotiations: 'since with the present threats it would be useful to reduce commitments in Flanders and apply our resources to other, more convenient, purposes. We may believe from the proceedings of the French that they will soon openly break with us' (**201** p. 103).

The failure of the negotiations meant that Olivares had to prepare for war with France while continuing to fight the Dutch. To make a new war appear 'just', he lent weight to the propaganda campaign being waged against France. Had not France invaded Italy and been disruptive in Germany? Had not Richelieu helped the Dutch? Was not the treaty of Bärwalde with Sweden an open challenge to Spain as well as the Emperor? He made a point of explaining to the Pope that 'the French are struggling all over Christendom on behalf of heresy' and that this needed to be opposed. Spain's offer of help to the Emperor against Sweden in the early 1630s was thus made with a view to it being reciprocated when war with France began. The peace of Prague of 1635 temporarily helped to stabilise the situation in central Europe and isolate France. Yet the military failures of 1636 left Spain once more a slave to the complexities of the wider-European conflicts, and her internal difficulties created insuperable problems for Olivares.

In Spain, the Catholic faith was universally adhered to, but the kingdoms other than Castile clung jealously to their political 'Liberties'. Olivares never succeeded in breaking down this federalist attitude and his attempts to harness the military and financial strength of all the kingdoms of the Peninsula brought Spain to the brink of disintegration. Thus, even though there was no internal religious challenge the unity of religious faith was not enough of a bond to hold Spain together. After Olivares' dismissal there seemed to be no dominating intelligence guiding Spain's affairs and she was humiliated by being left out of the Westphalian nego-tiations.

In terms of inter-state relations it can thus be argued that a major element in the Thirty Years War was not just the Protestant–Catholic division, but a conflict for hegemony *within* the various faiths. For instance, the battle for control of the Counter-Reformation, and the politically pre-eminent role in Europe that, it was assumed, would be the consequence of victory, ranged a Castile-dominated Spanish Catholicism against an anti-Habsburg French Catholicism, and an increasingly weakened Papal Catholic-ism. In many ways the treaty of Westphalia ensured that the movement for Catholic reform would not be the preserve of a single power bloc.

Thus, although religion and politics remained closely entwined in decision-making after 1648, the 'balance of exhaustion' which made possible the Westphalian agreements meant that the prin-ciples of confessional solidarity and dynastic Catholicism were subordinated to the need for a general peace. After 1648 rulers were less prepared to hazard fortune and territory for the sake of their faith. The logic of the European situation in 1648 was dictated by 'reasons of war'. The ever-increasing preoccupation of governments with the problem of finance led to the adoption of mercantilist theories which paid more attention to a country's wealth than its religion. Although religious disputes continued to influence political developments in industrial states, rulers ac-quired a more balanced view of inter-state relations which led to a slackening of religious passions, and a return to a period of 'little wars' and more manageable negotiations.

7 Military Developments

A military revolution?

From a military point of view it is possible to describe the developments of the period 1610 to 1628 as a change from 'little' wars to total war (**201**). There were many developments in military thinking and practice throughout Europe during the period of the Thirty Years War, but there has been much debate as to how far they were genuinely new or of lasting importance.

In 1956 M. Roberts examined many European changes in the art of war for the period 1560–1660 and concluded that in the four important areas of tactics, strategy, scale and size of armies, and the impact on society, there had been a 'Military Revolution' which 'stood like a divide separating medieval society from the modern world' (**62**).

According to Roberts, the important change in infantry tactics was the emergence of smaller units in linear formation firing salvoes, instead of the deployment of large pike squares. For the cavalry, the most common combat formation of the early seventeenth century was the *caracole* – a manoeuvre that combined a charge by successive ranks of horsemen and a discharge of weapons at thirty to fifty paces: each rank filed back to the rear of the formation to make way for following ranks who similarly charged, fired and filed back. Gradually this cumbersome method was replaced by the full-blown charge, which transformed the cavalry arm of the fighting forces. Both these developments required well trained and better disciplined troops, which led to the growth of standing armies. In strategic terms, several armies began to campaign simultaneously, with the result that the cautious and essentially defensive strategies of the preceding century were replaced by a more offensive spirit, with commanders seeking to bring on decisive battles. There were also important reforms in the use of artillery, not just for siege work but for faster-moving campaigns deep in enemy territory. Armies increased in size as a result of these developments and this forced changes in the way they were supplied and financed.

Roberts claimed that the really important developments stemmed from the reforms of the 'Dutch School' in the late sixteenth century – Maurice of Orange and his cousins William Louis and Count John II Nassau – and from those of Gustavus Adolphus in the seventeenth. Prior to the Dutch reforms 'tactics had withered, strategy had atrophied; and the men of the sixteenth century took refuge in firearms whose proper use they were still unable to compass, as an all too-simple answer to their military difficulties' (**192** p. 182). Yet it was Gustavus Adolphus who, 'with a firmer hand, a wider strategic vision, a more trenchant mind [and an extra generation of experience], was to take Maurice's methods, apply them, add to them and improve them, and in doing so was to impose upon the art of war a pattern which it retained almost unmodified until the advent of the revolutionary armies of France' (**192** p. 189).

In the light of more recent evidence G. Parker has questioned some of these conclusions about sixteenth-century tactical and strategic developments as well as the explanation given for the growth of military manpower. He still thinks that 'the scale of warfare in early modern Europe was revolutionised, and this had important and wide-ranging consequences' (**58** p. 103), but he is less impressed with the contributions of the Dutch and Swedish reforms to this process.

The Dutch reforms

In brief, the Dutch military reformers stressed better use of manpower, with shallower formations, reductions in the size of tactical units – but with increased numbers of officers, under-officers, musketeers and arquebusiers – and the importance of the countermarch whereby successive musketeer ranks advanced, fired and retired to re-load. They also advocated the massing of artillery to enable barrages to be employed at sieges; greater standardisation in weapon designs; the use of maps and field glasses; more attention to the training of soldiers and their discipline; and the need for regular and better pay for the troops.

Yet the majority of these developments were not new. The famous Spanish *tercio*, which was introduced as a tactical unit in 1534, had been reduced in size by the 1590's and its proportion of musketeers gradually increased. Cavalry tactics were hardly changed at all by the Dutch. Indeed, many of the interesting military developments of the early seventeenth century stemmed from the sixteenth-century Italian wars (**54** chs. 7–9), especially the *trace italienne* or bastion which strengthened fortifications in land warfare and led to many changes in military engineering and an increase in the size of armies for siege operations (**47** chs. 1–2). Though the Spanish–Dutch conflict produced some changes in fortress warfare, it has to be concluded that 'the Spanish and Dutch contributed in equal measure to the great advances that were made in fortress warfare in the last quarter of the sixteenth century. "The Method of Maurice of Nassau" with its labyrinthine siegeworks and its employment of soldier–pioneers was merely a continuation of what Parma had been doing in the 1580's' (**47** p. 89).

The campaigns of the renewed Spanish–Dutch conflict after 1621 lacked the innovative drive of the earlier struggle. The Spanish could not institutionalise their military experiences in the Netherlands and there was little in the way of continuity of thinking among their army personnel. For the Dutch, the 'conqueror of towns', Prince Frederick Henry, even with a French alliance from 1635, remained content to fight a defensive war with only minor inroads into Spanish Flanders.

Nor were those who tried to emulate Dutch tactics in Europe guaranteed success. Christian IV of Denmark was quickly forced to abandon the Hague Coalition at the hands of Tilly and Wallenstein. Frederick V and Christian of Brunswick lost battle after battle. Tilly and Spinola were never convinced that Dutch methods would produce results in areas where open–field warfare was demanded. The Spanish commanders made reforms where they saw positive advantages in doing so. For instance, Basta encouraged the reduction in numbers of the *tercio* in order to increase the frontage and reduce the depth of the formation and make it more flexible.

There were many ancillary services in operation before the Dutch reforms. In the 1530s new Spanish recruits were sent to Italy and North Africa before being posted to the Netherlands, in order to gain experience and basic training. There was also a special Spanish military treasury, a hierarchy of judicial courts, a system of medical care with resident doctors in every regiment, and a chaplain-general with a large number of chaplains acting under him. Many of these were also to be found in the Imperial armies of Wallenstein in the 1620s and 1630s. France and Italy had both developed a form of standing army as early as the fifteenth century and Maximilian 1 had intended the *Landsknechts* (created in 1497) to be a German equivalent.

The gradual improvements in the efficiency of firearms were not confined to one area of Europe. The breech-loader was replaced by the muzzle-loading gun in most armies; the developments in ballistics were likewise not confined to the Dutch (**52**); muskets were increasingly used beside the older arquebus, though the latter was still in use in some armies in the early battles of the Thirty Years War. As Parker points out '... wherever a situation of permanent or semi-permanent war existed, whether the Hundred Years War of the later Middle Ages, or the Thirty Years War of the seventeenth century, one finds, not surprisingly, standing armies, greater professionalism among the troops, improvements in military organisation and certain tactical innovations' (**58** p. 90–1).

Thus to think that the Dutch reforms created a military system that was entirely new and in every respect better than that of Renaissance Europe would be a mistake. Certainly the war between Spain and the Netherlands was a sound training ground for many of the commanders of the Thirty Years War and the English civil war (**61**). It is also true that the Dutch moves of 1595 towards standardisation and uniformity in the size and calibre of weapons were of lasting importance to the conduct of war. The many military training manuals, encouraged by John Nassau and bearing fruit in the books of Jacob de Gheyn and Jacob von Wallhausen, were likewise important contributions to the art of war in early modern Europe. Yet generally speaking by 1630 the Dutch reforms had not been fully appraised in all aspects of warfare and their full implications had not been worked out. 'New' methods existed side by side with older ones even in Dutch armies, and more than one commander could hit upon almost the same device for solving problems that were faced by all.

Gustavus Adolphus

The claims of originality made for Gustavus Adolphus are similarly open to doubt. It is true that in tactical terms the Swedish King restored to the cavalry and infantry the capacity to attack as well as defend – by abandoning the *caracole* manoeuvre; he intensified the firepower of all sections of the army – especially by changing firing formations and introducing lighter weapons; he emphasised increased mobility especially in the artillery – where the 'regimental' four-pounder cannon was introduced; he combined different sections of his armies; and he attempted to develop self-reliance in his officer corps and through them in his troops generally. Yet it still seems generous for Roberts to claim that 'in him is incarnate the military revolution' (**192** p. 270).

Gustavus always had difficulty raising a full levy for his squadrons, and the shortfall in recruits forced him to develop a smaller unit – the field regiment – as well as to hire more mercenaries. Those who argue that Sweden established the first professional national army in this period would do well to recall that at Breitenfeld the Swedes totalled only 20 per cent of the army, and at Lützen only 18 percent (**194** p. 44).

As with the Dutch reformers, Gustavus Adolphus did little to improve cavalry equipment, and although he emphasised a combination of foot and horse to give the cavalry a more offensive role, it is perhaps more realistic to say that it was the successes of Condé and Turenne, in the later battles of the Thirty Years War, that really established the cavalry charge as a major element in military success. Even Gustavus' obsession with reducing the weight of field guns for extra mobility had been pre-dated by the Dutch and Spanish armies, and the increase in mobility was often achieved at the expense of efficiency. It is significant that his successors began to cast heavier guns for the later campaigns of the Thirty Years War.

It may be true to say that Gustavus' successes in Germany ensured the triumph of the linear order, but the decrease in size of armies after the death of Wallenstein led to an increasing rigidity in linear tactics. In military terms it is difficult to see what the famous Swedish victories of Breitenfeld, Lützen, Wittstock and Jankow actually achieved. Fighting in Europe was not brought to an abrupt end and the two battles that came nearest to being truly decisive – White Mountain in 1620 and Nördlingen in 1634 – were actually Imperial Spanish victories. In the short term the arbitration of battle in early modern Europe was not final nor definitive.

In terms of strategy, Gustavus was limited by the need to feed his expanding army and by the weight of his artillery. By the spring of 1631, his army had increased in size from 10,000 to 100,000, and this forced Gustavus to march into the richest area in Germany, around Mainz, for the following winter. He also needed to be near navigable waterways so that his artillery could be transported easily. The demands of logistics thus seem to have had more influence on Swedish strategy than tactical development (**16** pp. 12–17). Gustavus was unable to remain long in any area and he was constantly on the move in search of food and supplies. The political crisis in the Swedish command after 1632 was mainly due to lack of supplies, and led to a fall in morale and mass desertions by mercenaries.

It is fair to say that Gustavus encouraged, developed and transformed many progressive tendencies found in other systems. Of all the commanders he came nearest to developing the tactic that, for the circumstances of the time, best combined hitting power, mobility and defensive strength. Yet in all these aspects he typified rather than transcended the practices of his time.

Wallenstein

Wallenstein shared many of Gustavus' administrative and logistical problems. By the summer of 1631 Wallenstein had some 54 regiments of foot and 75 regiments of horse, a total well in excess of 100,000 men under his command. As with Gustavus, recruitment was based on set areas and never provided sufficient men to meet Wallenstein's tactical requirements – Mann thinks he should have had some 237,000 men in 1632 (**55**). Many of the states of the Empire wanted to avoid the heavy fiscal burdens which a hostile foreign policy required and this severely limited imperialist plans. In 1625 it cost something like 500,000 gulden to raise an infantry regiment of 3,000 men, and Emperor Ferdinand was forced to depend on others besides the Estates to raise men for him.

It has been estimated that for Germany alone between 1631 and 1634 there were about 300 independent military enterprises or 'entrepreneurs' making money out of raising troops (**61**). Some, like the minor gentry, raised only single companies or squadrons, but Wallenstein, as Imperial Commander-in-chief and Duke of Friedland, raised whole armies. At the beginning of the Thirty Years War he had offered the Emperor the use of his single Moravian regiment. After an advantageous marriage to a daughter of the wealthy Count Harrach (1623) and receipt of profits from minting sub-standard coins in Bohemia, he was able to raise an army in 1625. He was quickly promoted to Commander-in-chief of the Imperial armies, and in 1628 was granted full authority for recruitment of troops and for the appointment and promotion of all officers up to the rank of colonel. Each colonel was given patents entitling him to recruit ten battalions and to select his own officers, who were in turn given permission to raise men.

The great majority of regiments were kept on active service after 1626, and this forced Wallenstein to demand more financial help from the Emperor. He had been prepared to raise 50,000 men for Ferdinand, but not to keep them as well. Those who criticised Wallenstein for not following up the slogging match of Dessau Bridge, or for not pressing for a decisive victory in the Hungarian campaign, got the reply that while the Dutch, Swedes and English remained in the coalition against him and had control of the sea, 'the war will have to be fed with gold and silver from the Indies and perchance continued for thirty years before something salutary may ensue' (**55** p. 297).

As the army grew in size so did the financial demands made by Wallenstein. It has been estimated that the wars fought between 1618 and 1648 by Imperial armies alone cost 110 million gulden, 28 million of which had been required during Wallenstein's two periods of command. In all, with monies paid to allied princes for their armies, the figure may have been 250 million gulden. Spain provided only 1,700,000 gulden over the whole period and the Popes managed only 900,000. Thus the great bulk of the costs had to be borne by the Imperial exchequer and the hereditary lands. This helps to explain why the system of 'contributions', which had initially been employed by Buquoy and Spinola, had to be applied more forcefully by Wallenstein (**60**).

Wallenstein's Imperial Commissioners, who had the duty of extracting the contributions, were never welcomed and often feared. Wallenstein also had the help of far-reaching credit relations which extended to Vienna, Augsburg, Nuremberg, Hamburg, Amsterdam and Antwerp. His agents hoped to turn the fairs in Frankfurt and Leipzig and the markets of Linz and Vienna into clearing houses for the Imperial commanders and their rapacious officers, whose dual intent of making quick fortunes and financing war pushed the average cost per soldier higher than it was to be in the nineteenth century (**23** p. 159).

Yet Wallenstein's activities did not go uncriticised. Maximilian of Bavaria in particular feared what this over-mighty subject, with his huge army, might do next [**doc. 11**]. Wallenstein's own motto, *invita invidia* – 'envy defying' – appeared a challenge in its own right. Yet he had always been aware of the hostility his policies created, and his letters to the Emperor are full of biting criticisms of his opponents. Despite the victories of the 1627 campaign and the extension of his own personal authority with the acquisition of Mecklenburg, the 'General of the whole Imperial Armada as well as Admiral of the Atlantic and Baltic Seas' never lost sight of the realities of war. The *almirantazgo* policy, if followed to its conclusions, might have succeeded in bringing peace to the Empire and the defeat of the Dutch, but Wallenstein was always doubtful that the Spaniards could defeat the Dutch, and the Swedish invasion reminded him that logistically the Emperor could afford only defensive war. The resources for achieving a decisive victory were simply not available.

Yet Wallenstein knew that the powers opposing him were similarly poorly placed economically and financially to defeat his large army and that the prospect for Europe was a series of *ad hoc* campaigns designed to create a suitable balance of exhaustion, leading to a general peace. For that type of war Wallenstein was certainly well prepared. Schiller was not far wrong when he wrote that 'the war was only continued to provide work and bread for the troops, that by and large one argued only about the advantages of the winter quarters and that the finding of good accommodation for the army was more highly esteemed than the winning of a major battle' (**23** p. 159).

After the deaths of Gustavus Adolphus and Wallenstein, both the Swedish and Imperial commanders were forced to develop and refine the tactical innovations of the previous period and the French began to concentrate on the problems of logistics. Europe could no longer support large armies. Baner, Torstensson and Wrangel were never able to muster more than 15,000 men at any single point and, despite Baner's innovation at Wittstock, where his army operated in two independent groups, the question of supplies threatened to reduce the art of war to a series of deep cavalry charges against towns. Torstensson's rapid marches have become famous, but they were initiated by the demands of logistics: hence his attempts to prune anything that reduced mobility. His development of an independent artillery arm, which combined so successfully with cavalry charges at Jankow, was certainly productive of new artillery tactics after the Thirty Years War, but at the time was an attempt to free troop movements from river lines. Even so, despite the efforts of the Frenchman Le Tellier to introduce a more professional provisioning system, by the end of the Thirty Years War no army had a permanent reserve, and stores amassed for any operation were normally on a single campaign basis.

However, over the period 1470 to 1700, despite the reductions of the later years of the Thirty Years War, there was a tenfold increase in the total numbers of armed forces in the pay of leading European states (**58** p. 96):

Date	Spanish Monarchy	Dutch Republic	France	England	Sweden
1470s	20,000		40,000	25,000	
1550s	150,000		50,000	20,000	
1590s	200,000	20,000	80,000	30,000	15,000
1630s	300,000	50,000	150,000		45,000
1650s	100,000		100,000	70,000	70,000
1670s	70,000	110,000	120,000		63,000
1700s	50,000	100,000	400,000	87,000	100,000

This increase pre-dated the Dutch reforms. The Spanish army of Flanders was already 86,000 strong in 1574 when Maurice was only six years old. With the decline of heavy cavalry units, the use of pikemen in offensive situations increased the numbers of infantrymen in armies and they were easier to recruit, arm and train. Also, the *trace italienne* made siegework far more difficult and this in turn called for increased numbers of footsoldiers.

The 'Age of Discovery' witnessed an increase in expeditions for trade, war and piracy, especially after the 1590s when the Dutch began to make serious inroads into the Spanish–Portuguese empires. These developments forced the maritime nations to strengthen their flotillas and ports and add further tiers of guns to warships, all of which served to enlarge their fighting forces.

However, despite the general increase in wealth during the sixteenth century, most governments could not pay for major and prolonged wars out of current taxation. The need to finance military activity normally led governments to spend money in advance of revenue by way of loans, and this often caused domestic problems. When the flow of cash to troops was reduced, armies faced discipline problems and desertions. To that extent the Thirty Years War was more a struggle for resources than the highpoint of the military revolution. Governments gambled 'as to which tottering conglomeration of alienated local interests and exhausted taxpayers could avoid collapsing for longer than its enemies' so that the longer the war lasted 'the more necessary it seemed for the temporarily stronger party in the [peace] negotiations to secure some real gain, hence the difficulty of reaching any real settlement' (**16** IV, ch. 1). The Thirty Years War could not be terminated by a single battle or a dashing campaign or the use of some new tactic and to that extent it reveals the shortcomings of the military 'revolution' more than the strengths.

Part Four: Assessment

8 Conclusions

Over the past ninety years there have been a number of revisions of traditional assumptions about the first half of the seventeenth century, and of the Thirty Years War in particular. Most of these new interpretations agree that the war must be considered a continent-wide phenomenon which influenced the history of international relations as well as the internal affairs of most European states. Yet the 'revisionists' do not agree on all matters, and many of their contentions raise more questions than can as yet be satisfactorily answered.

The first casualty in the process of re-interpretation has been the view that the War was specifically a German affair, based on religious divisions, which gradually spread to involve other European powers. S. H. Steinberg, for instance, doubts whether this old conception of the Thirty Years War retains any value for the historian. He thinks it imparts a false unity to the conflicts that were either already in existence by 1618 or developed afterwards (**44**). He argues that there was no single war but a series of intermittent wars beginning in 1609 with the Jülich-Cleves succession conflict and ending with the peace of the Pyrenees in 1659. In his view these wars were not basically religious or manifestations of a German civil war, but rather a series of struggles for control of central Europe. He suggests that each conflict has to be studied as a significant historical occurrence in its own right and that it is no longer useful to make the accounts of these crises fit into a wider thesis that has lost its explanatory power.

However Steinberg underestimates Germany's role as a catalyst for other European conflicts. It is possible to argue that each crisis was a subtle blend of local and international issues and that some of these conflicts, and especially those in Germany, had more significance in shaping the course of events in Europe generally than others. It may be that by 1618 it was the enmity of Bourbon and Habsburg, coupled with the increasing likelihood that Spain would not renew her truce with the Dutch rebels after 1621, that claimed the attention of most European statesmen. Yet it still seems right to conclude with C. V. Wedgwood that 'the arch of European politics rested on the keystone of Germany' (**41** p. 33). Spain wanted to control the Rhine to secure her lines of communication from Itaɪy to the Netherlands; France and the Dutch rebels wanted to break the Spanish Road at various points; Sweden and Denmark were competing for control of the north German coastline on the Baltic; the Pope and France were trying to create a 'third force' in Germany to combat the influence of the Habsburgs on the Catholic reform movement; and the instability of the northern Italian states attracted the attentions not just of France and Spain, but also of Austria. It is difficult to deny that the revolt in Prague and the action of Frederick V of the Palatinate were crucial events in bringing about the onset of a Europe-wide war.

Other historians critical of the older accounts of the Thirty Years War dislike their emphasis on political, military and diplomatic developments at the expense of what they consider to be deeper and more fundamental social and economic tensions in early modern Europe.

Polisensky thinks that 'the political conflict, commonly called the Thirty Years War, was the logical outcome of the crisis of policy of the old feudal ruling class. This political crisis had deep social and economic roots' (**32** p. 37). For Polisensky, and other Marxist historians, the Thirty Years War can be seen as a contest for power springing from the whole course of European economic and social evolution in the sixteenth and seventeenth centuries. New accounts of the war must, therefore, be based on an analysis of the social structure of both sides, the Habsburg–Catholic camp and the anti-Habsburg 'Great Coalition'. In Polisensky's view, such an examination would support the view that the war arose out of a 'critical social and economic situation' in Europe, but especially in Bohemia.

Certainly the immediate 'trigger' for the revolt in Bohemia was the threat posed by the political and social implications of the Catholic reform movement under Rudolf II and Ferdinand II to the material interests of the Protestant nobility (**16** pp. 503–30). Yet Polisensky also claims that the revolt was, *in essence*, a conflict between an embryonic 'bourgeois' society and a feudal-Catholic one, and that it mirrored a Europe-wide conflict of two conceptions of life and society. While it is possible to say that there was a fear of what the consequences of Habsburg imperialism might entail in terms of economic dislocation and dispossession, it is difficult to maintain that the economic aspect of anti-Habsburg feeling was paramount. Though there were competing conceptions of life in seventeenth-century Europe, it is not clear that there were just two, and that the major distinction was economic.

Supporters of the economic argument have suggested that contemporaries in Bohemia viewed the Church as an economic power in religious guise and that the struggle to defend the 'Letter of Majesty' was really a struggle to defend the wealth that ecclesiastical possessions bequeathed. Yet even if this contention is accepted, it is not sufficient to justify Polisensky's claim that the Bohemian revolt was a conflict between a 'bourgeois' society and a 'feudal' one. In any case, it is difficult to support the view that the 'Letter of Majesty' *was* an economic document in the sense intended. Neither is it possible to justify the claim that the social situation in Bohemia was a microcosm of a European economic and social system that was experiencing an acute crisis, since the thesis of a general crisis in seventeenth-century Europe is itself open to criticism.

Certainly the character and organisation of Habsburg government in Bohemia radicalised sections of the nobility, but there had been a history of opposition to the Catholic régime based on Hussite and Reformed humanist traditions, and it is difficult to establish that the revolt in 1618 was the product of a Bohemian society in a state of *exceptional* crisis. The aristocratic leaders failed to break down the particularism of individual crown lands, and their unwillingness to grant the Bohemian citizens and peasants a share in the rights they won for themselves in 1609 led to the alienation of these groups when their support would have been invaluable in 1618. The revolt was not, therefore, a kingdom-wide civil war or revolution.

Yet the revolt was not insignificant. The Habsburgs could not afford to let the crown fall into the hands of a Protestant ruler. Bohemia gave the Habsburgs the potential to exercise great influence in Germany and central Europe, especially since it controlled major trade routes and was an important source of wealth. The fact that the revolt led to the subjugation of Bohemia, a Catholic take-over in the Palatinate, and a heightening of tension in the politically sensitive areas of the Rhineland, means that the historian cannot ignore its role in initiating the chain of events that led to the European war. Since economic, social and political issues were inextricably intertwined, Polisensky's emphasis on the economic and social aspects leads to an unbalanced rationale of the period.

However, some of the traditional claims made for the significance of the Thirty Years War certainly need revising. The view that the war and the peace treaty marked the end of an epoch and paved the way for the decline of Spain and the greatness of France needs qualifying. It is difficult to apply the concept of 'decline' to Spain before 1659 (**149**), and France's ascendancy in Europe was not assured by the treaty of Westphalia. Another questionable claim is that the war discredited the Emperor's authority in Germany. It can equally be argued that Ferdinand III's power was not any more negligible than that of Ferdinand I, Rudolf, or Matthias. Only in contrast with the temporary ascendancy enjoyed by Ferdinand II in 1629 did Habsburg power appear to have been weakened. Similarly, the idea that secular self-interest replaced religious standards in public life after 1648 needs to be handled with care. It is difficult to assess the role of religious zeal in political behaviour. In some respects after 1648 the significance of issues of national security, and commercial and dynastic ambitions, came to have more prominence as reasons for waging war than the defence of the faith. Yet politics and religion had been closely entwined throughout the conflict and 'reasons of state' and 'reasons of war' had often been paramount. There was no sudden secularisation of public life.

In economic and social terms the war was not the great disaster that some German historians have claimed. However, it would be wrong to assume that all the contemporary accounts of economic ruin and misery were exaggerated. The fighting certainly made recovery very difficult and its effects were damaging to many occupations and enterprises. The financial demands of war created many fiscal, political and social pressures for the majority of governments. The progression of sieges and campaigns, with the attendant scourges of plague, famine and slaughter, brought misery to many people. Even though the main fighting was limited to Bohemia and Austria, the Rhineland, the Black Forest and the Saxon plain, troop movements spread fear into many districts. It mattered little whether the soldiers over-running an area were friendly or not, since they all had to be supported at the expense of the inhabitants.

It is true that by the end of the Thirty Years War, 'Contributions' were well on the way to being ritualised, with local communities becoming adept at calculating an army's demands in order to avoid unnecessary plunder and destruction. War could bring guaranteed prices, ready markets, even new industrial and manufacturing opportunities. Thus money lost through contributions often found its way back into the local community, especially where the procedure of trade–barter–trade was well developed. Indeed, beyond the mercenaries and *Condottieri*, many local people came to rely on war for their livelihood. Yet this cannot disguise the misery that the kidnappings, ransoms, outright expropriation, and physical destruction of the fighting brought to the vast majority of people in the war zones. Once it was realised that the fighting could not be terminated by a single victory or a brilliant feat of arms, a general cynicism helped to create a depressing war psychology which perceived life as being nasty, brutish and short. Camerarius echoed this view towards the end of the war when he lamented: 'Happy are they who in this wretched time are already asleep in the Lord' (**139** p. 3).

Wedgwood thinks the war was 'confused in its causes, devious in its course, futile in its result' (**41** p. 460). There is some truth in that conclusion. In many ways the situation established in the Empire in 1648 was essentially that of 1618. If the fighting had ended in 1623, 1629, or 1635, the Habsburgs would have been in a much stronger position. As it was, there were only a few major changes. Western Pomerania and Alsace were in foreign hands in 1648, Brandenburg, Saxony and Bavaria had increased their territory, the Elector Palatine had lost much of his and the Habsburgs had strengthened their control of Bohemia. Thus the peace of Westphalia had brought Germany full circle. The Catholic powers had hoped to regain the land secularised since 1559, the Emperor wanted to re-establish his authority over the princes and estates, Sweden sought to create a new Evangelical Germanic Federation, but none of these aims had been secured. The peace did not even interfere with the constitution of Germany in *detail*; this was to be the work of the next German Diet – although, when it began in 1653, the Habsburgs were able to prevent serious challenges to their authority.

Many of the powers outside the Empire had still to settle disputes left over from the war period. Spain remained at war with France and had suffered losses in north Italy, the Netherlands and the Rhineland. France was bankrupt in 1648 and could not claim hegemony in Europe until after 1659. Sweden had many internal troubles to deal with after 1648 as well as a conflict with Brandenburg. The Great Elector of Brandenburg won a great military victory against the Swedes at Fehrbellin in 1675, and he constantly prodded Sweden's territory in northern Germany. These disputes gradually weakened Sweden's capacity to resist the later threat of Russian expansion into the Baltic. Thus it is quite possible to claim that the treaties of the Pyrenees and Oliva were more of a turning-point in European history than the treaty of Westphalia.

However, the term 'Thirty Years War' is still of value to historians. Certainly the sense of terminology depends on who is using it. It is clear that the 'Thirty Years War' is correct when applied to Germany and incorrect when applied to the other European conflicts of the period. Yet the issues involved in the various disputes were so complex that to use any one of the conflicts to describe the welter of events in Europe in the first half of the seventeenth century merely obscures the important linkages and continuities that existed between them. Even contemporaries described these developments as being part of a Thirty Years War (**167**). For roughly thirty years the major powers were involved in Europe's first all-embracing conflagration. They fought on German soil often for issues which were not concerned with Germany alone, but Germany's problems acted as a catalyst. The various governments were committed to a series of campaigns they could do little to control individually, and when the essentially German peace of Westphalia had been negotiated it is significant that the remaining conflicts lacked the potency to renew the general European war. To that extent 1648 remains an important turning point in European relations.

Thus, rather than relegate the Thirty Years War to the dustbin of history, the historian has to reinterpret it as a major phenomenon in *European* history. Polisensky is right when he reminds students of the period that '... it was no accident that from the second half of the sixteenth century the Spanish silver fleets from America carried with them the hopes and fears even of far-off Bohemia. American silver for the Spaniards, East Indian spices for the Dutch and the English, the struggles to shut off or keep open the Baltic and the Mediterranean, Turkish dominion of the Balkans: all these are reflected in one way or another in the documents of this first conflict of, as it were, world-wide proportions' (**133**).

Part Five: Documents

The truce between Spain and the Netherlands

Clause four of the truce between Spain and the Netherlands agreed in 1607 and confirmed by Madrid in 1609. This proved one of the more contentious clauses of the agreement:

The subjects and inhabitants of the countries of the said lord king, archdukes and estates shall have good relations and friendship with one another during the said Truce, without resenting the damage and harm that they have received in the past; they shall also be able to enter and to stay in one another's countries, and to exercise there their trade and commerce in full security both by sea and other waters as well as by land; however the said king understands this to be restrained and limited to the kingdoms, countries, lands and lordships which he has and possesses in Europe and other places and seas in which the subjects of other princes who are his friends and allies have the said trade by mutual consent; as regards the places, towns, ports and harbours that he holds beyond the said limits, that the lords estates and their subjects may not carry on any trade without the express permission of the said lord king; but they shall be allowed to carry on the said trade, if it seems good to them, in the countries of all other princes, potentates and peoples who may wish to permit them to do so even outside the said limits, without the said lord king, his officers and subjects who depend on him making any impediment in this event to the said princes, potentates and peoples who may have permitted it to them, nor equally to them [ie the Dutch] or to the persons with whom they have carried out or will carry out the said trade.

J. Dumont, *Corps Universel Diplomatique de Droit de Gens*, vol. v, part 2, Amsterdam, 1728, pp. 99–102; cited in (**163**), pp. 278–9.

document 2

The Counter-Reformation in Austria

Religious grievance and wartime violence. The word 'Dutch' here means 'German' (Deutsch).

Two very lamentable relations: The one, the grievances for religion, of those of Stiria, Carinthia, and Crayne, under Ferdinand then Duke of Gratz, now Emperour. The other, the now present most humble supplication, of certayne of the states of Lower Austria, unto the said Emperour. Wherein is shewed the most terrible, inhumane, and barbarian tyrannies, commited by the Emperour's soldiers, specially the Casockes and Wallons, in the said countrie. Done out of the Dutch and printed 1620.

... To declare to the World the hourely and minutely griefe of Conscience and grievances for the Religion which wee have had, were almost impossible and also unnecessary, since it is alas, too well knowne to this Land, to the Empire, and to a great part of the World; yet neverthelesse we will rehearse a few.

1. First, by priviledge, and good will of the illustrious Arch-Duke Charles of Austria, of famous memory, our gracious Lord and Prince, was granted to the professors of the Gospell, many special Ministers in the principall Townes as in Gratz, Indenburgk, Clagenfourt, and Labach.

2. Item, their Colledges and free Schooles of learning, for instructing Noblemens, and other Children, were admitted and granted them, in the foresaid Townes ... all which priviledges are most violently taken from them.

3. Item, in the Countrey of Stiria, were many Cathedrall and other Parish Churches also violently taken from them.

4. Also many priviledged Churches, pulled downe, and blowne up with Gunpowder.

5. One hundred Preachers and Ministers commanded upon paine of death to depart the province of Stiria.

6. A great many more Schoole-masters, and Teachers of the Youth, most pittifully banished.

7. Item, many Church-yards, and resting places for the dead bodyes of the faithfull, being walled and paled about, were most barbously pulled downe, and made levell with the ground.

8. The bodies of the faithfull digged up, and given to be devoured by Dogs and Hogs; as also the Coffins taken and set by the highway side, some burnt with fire; a worke both barbarous and inhumane.

9. Also upon the burial-places of the faithful, were erected Gibets and places for execution of malefactors. Also upon those places where Protestant Churches stood, or where the Pulpit stood, or the Frone-stone, were erected alwaies most filthy spectacles most ugly to behold...

11. Moreover, (a griefe above all griefes) many thousands that professed the Gospell, were most cruelly and shamefully tormented and tortured, and by the same torments compelled shamefully, to denie and renounce the truth of Christs Evangell...

Most gracious Prince, the unspeakable spoyling, destruction, miserie, trouble, calamitie, and subiection of these countries, wrought and effected by the accursed Cosackes and others your Maiesties Souldiers brought into the same, together with the robbings, murtherings, sackings, burnings, massacrings, and other barbarian cruelties used and committed therein, mooveth and provoketh us in the name and behalfe of our principall Lords and the whole Countrey, to take and have our recourse, next unto God, to your Emperiall Maiestie, with sighes and teares to renew our former complaints...

So it is, and it pleased your Imperial Maiesty, that for as much, as the Wallons, and other strange Souldiers, brought into this Country, cease not continually, to make a common practise to waste, spoyle, burne, murther, and massacre the Countrie and the Commons thereof ... sparing not to burne whole Villages, Hamlets, and Market-townes, and in them Storehouses for the provision of Widdowes and Orphans ... seised upon, spoyled, and burnt their Castles, houses, and their provision for their houses, being taken from them, the poore subiects that are employed about necessary defences, cannot get a bit of bread to relieve themselves withall, but are constrained to starve and die for hunger. Boys and Women being fearfully violated and ravished, are carried prisoners away, both young and old men and women, most cruelly and terribly martired, tortured, prest, and their flesh pinsht, and pulled from their bodies with burning tongues, hanged up by the necks, hands, feete, and their privy-members, women, gentlewomen, and young wenches under yeeres ravished till they die, women great with child, layd so long upon the fire, untill which time as that men may see the fruit in their bodies, and so both mother and child die together, old and young, high and low status, spiritual and temporal persons, without difference....

Macartney (**6**), pp. 13–22.

document 3

The Letter of Majesty of July, 1609

We, Rudolf etc., make known this Patent to all men, to be kept in mind forever:

All three Estates of Our Kingdom of Bohemia who receive the body and blood of Our Lord Jesus Christ in both Kinds, Our beloved and loyal subjects, have at the Diets held in the Castle of Prague in the past year of the Lord 1608 on the Monday after Exaudi and on the Friday after the Feast of John the Baptist in the same year, humbly and with due submissiveness besought Us, as Kings of Bohemia: that the general Bohemian Confession, called by some the Augsburg Confession, which was codified at the general Diet of 1575 and submitted to His Majesty the Emperor Maximilian of glorious and honoured memory, Our most beloved father ... and the settlement between them [ie between the neo-Utraquists and the Bohemian Brothers] contained in the foreword to the same Confession, and also the other requests relating to religion, expressly added by them at the same Diet, may be confirmed, the free practice of the Christian religion in both Kinds permitted without let or hindrance, and sufficient assurances be given to the Estates by Us...

Firstly, as it is already laid down in the Bohemian Constitution in respect of the faiths of one or both Kinds, that no man shall vex another, but rather that all shall hold together as good friends ... this article shall be constantly observed, and both parties shall be held in future to respect it...

Furthermore, We wish to show the Utraquist Estates Our especial favour, and to restore to their authority and keeping the lower Prague Consistory, and We also most graciously concede that the Utraquist Estates may renew the said Consistory with its clergy according to their faith and associations, and also have their preachers, both Bohemian and German, ordained accordingly ... without any hindrance from the Archbishop of Prague, or any person ... We do will and particularly enjoin that, for the preservation of amity and concord, each party shall practise its religion freely and without restriction, subject to the governance and direction of its own clergy, and that neither party shall impose any rules on the other in respect of its religion or usages, neither prevent the practice of its religion, interment of bodies in churches or graveyards, or tolling of bells.

·As from today, no person, neither of the higher free Estates nor the inhabitants of unfree towns and villages, nor the peasants, shall be forced or compelled by any device by the authorities over them or by any person, spiritual or temporal, to forsake his religion and accept another religion.

Macartney (**6**), pp. 22–30.

document 4
The Edict of Restitution, 1629

We, Ferdinand, by the grace of God, Holy Roman Emperor, etc., are determined for the realization both of the religious and profane peace to despatch our Imperial commissioners into the Empire; to reclaim all the archbishoprics, bishoprics, prelacies, monasteries, hospitals and endowments which the Catholics had possessed at the time of the Treaty of Passau [1552] and of which they have been illegally deprived; and to put into all these Catholic foundations duly qualified persons so that each may get his proper due. We herewith declare that the Religious Peace [of 1555] refers only to the Augsburg Confession as it was submitted to our ancestor Emperor Charles V on 25 June 1530; and that all other doctrines and sects, whatever names they may have, not included in the Peace are forbidden and cannot be tolerated. We therefore command to all and everybody under punishment of the religious and the land ban that they shall at once cease opposing our ordinance and carry it out in their lands and territories and also assist our commissioners. Such as hold the archbishoprics and bishoprics, prelacies, monasteries, hospitals, etc., shall forthwith return them to our Imperial commissioners with all their appurtenances. Should they not carry out this behest they will not only expose themselves to the Imperial ban and to the immediate loss of all their privileges and rights without any further sentence or condemnation, but to the inevitable real execution of that order and be distrained by force.

Cited in Benecke (**13**), p. 14 from E. Reich (ed), *Select Documents Illustrating Medieval and Modern History'* (**8**).

document 5

The Treaty of Bärwalde, January 1631

[After a preamble]

Between Their Most Serene Majesties the Kings of Sweden and France there shall be an alliance for the defence of the friends of each and both of them, for the safeguarding of the Baltic and Oceanic Seas, the liberty of commerce, and the restitution of the oppressed States of the Roman Empire; and also in order to ensure that the fortress and defence-works which have been constructed, in the ports and on the shores of the Baltic and Oceanic Seas, and in the Grisons, be demolished and reduced to the state in which they were immediately before this present German war. And because up to the present the enemy has refused to give a just reparation for the injuries he has caused, and has hitherto rejected all appeals, [the allies] take up arms to vindicate the cause of their common friends. To that end the King of Sweden ... will at his own expense bring to and maintain in Germany 30,000 foot and 6000 heavy-armed cavalry. The King of France will contribute 400,000 Imperial *Thaler*, that is, a million *livres tournois*, every year, which will be paid and accounted for without fail to the agents of the King of Sweden deputed for that purpose, either at Paris or Amsterdam, as the King of Sweden may find the more convenient; whereof one half to be paid on 15 May, and the other on 15 November each year. The raising of soldiers and sailors, the sale of ships and materials of war, are to be free as between the territories of the allies, but are to be refused to enemies ... If God should be pleased to grant successes to the King of Sweden, he is in matters of religion to treat territories occupied by or ceded to him according to the laws and customs of the Empire; and in places where the exercise of the Roman Catholic religion exists, it shall remain undisturbed. Any other States or Princes, as well within Germany as without, who may wish to accede to this league, shall be admitted to it ... With the Duke of Bavaria and the Catholic League friendship, or at least neutrality, is to be preserved, provided that they on their side observe it. And if, by the grace of God, an opportunity to treat for peace should present itself, the negotiations shall be conducted jointly by the allies, and neither will without the other initiate or conclude a peace. This alliance shall last for five years ...; if a sure peace is not obtained within that time, it may be further extended by agreement of the allies. It is agreed, finally, that since negotiations for this alliance began last year, and the King of Sweden has in the meanwhile been at great expense for this war, for this first year, which is now almost elapsed, 300,000 *livres tournois*, that is, 120,000 Imperial *Thaler*, shall be furnished in the name of the King of France on the day of the signature of this present treaty....

Roberts (**9**), pp. 136–37).

document 6
The League of Heilbronn, April 1633

First, the Princes and Estates who have met here with the Crown of Sweden under the guidance of the Royal Swedish Chancellor [Axel Oxenstierna] freely agree to join together in alliance [*Confoederieren*] and give each other mutual aid in order that the freedom of Germany [*Teutsch Libertät*] and also observance of the statutes and laws of the Holy Roman Empire shall once again be observed, and that the restitution of the Protestant Estates' rights in matters secular and religious shall be kept in a safely concluded peace. Furthermore, the Crown of Sweden is to have compensation [satisfaction], and all the separate alliances that the Crown of Sweden has made with individual Princes and Estates in the four Upper Circles of the Empire [that is, the Protestant Estates of the Electoral–Rhenish, Franconian, Swabian and Upper–Rhenish Circles] shall continue to be upheld in all points and not be suspended but rather extended. Such separate alliances shall instead enhance the strength of this confederation by impressing on every member the importance of and need for each and every one's full contributions to be rendered to it.

Second, because an effective wartime alliance needs leadership, so the Crown of Sweden under the guidance of Chancellor Oxenstierna has agreed to accept the same on the demand of the assembled confederates....

Third, that to help the Chancellor, a council of well qualified persons shall be appointed to organize the forces of the confederates and of the Circles....

Fourth, no confederate member shall enter into any separate negotiations with the enemy unless it is with the prior consent of the Chancellor and fellow confederates. All such matters shall be brought before the confederate council and the assemblies of the Circles.

Fifth, if any confederate tries to make his own policy [*gefaehrlicher*

Practicem] such as becoming neutral, then when he is under threat or attack from the enemy, he shall not receive aid from the confederation....

Sixth, it is agreed that for the duration of the war and until an agreed peace can be achieved, the confederates in the four Circles shall keep armies properly supplied with money, food, ammunition and artillery [*Gelt, Viures, ammunition vund Artillerie*]....

Seventh, in order that the war may be waged more effectively, strict army discipline shall be enforced and all excesses are to be prevented. The troops are to be regularly supplied with field treasuries and depots.

Eighth, the Chancellor has promised to consult his council and provide military reforms, restrain the regiments that have caused trouble and restore discipline in order that commerce may flourish once more among the ordinary people who will then be able to earn their living again. The Estates shall have their powers of jurisdiction and police restored and all extortions, billets and route marches shall henceforth be strictly supervised. As far as possible the local authorities shall have power to assign billets and all the Estates shall have supervisory power over the ways and means of paying the soldiers quartered on them in their localities.

Benecke (**13**), pp. 14–15.

document 7
The Peace of Prague, 1635

3. Concerning all the ecclesiastical lands and properties that lay within territorial state jurisdiction and that were already secularized before the agreement at Passau [of 1552] by the Electors and Imperial Estates who are members of the Augsburg Confession [Lutherans], they shall all remain according to the clear letter and direction of the established, highly esteemed religious peace [of 1555].

4. However, concerning the ecclesiastical lands and properties that were territorial states in their own right, and that were secularized before the agreement at Passau, as well as all those ecclesiastical lands and properties that have fallen into the hands of members of the Augsburg Confession after the conclusion of the Passau agreement, whether they lay within territorial state jurisdiction or were territorial states in their own right, we have finally agreed that those Electors and Imperial Estates who held these

lands on 12 November 1627, new style, shall have complete and free control of the same for a period of forty years from the date of this concluded agreement. And any authority that has been deprived of such lands since 12 November 1627 shall have them returned, yet without any right to claim costs or damages.

74. To achieve the long-desired pacification of our dear fatherland of the German nation ... each and every military occupation, recruiting and mustering, war tax and other grievance against the laws of the Empire, with which the Empire has recently been burdened, is in future to cease entirely, and is never to be enforced again.

75. In like manner there shall never be another particular military constitution set up within the Empire, be it from the head or members, that goes against the Emperor's coronation oath, the laws of the Empire, and of the Imperial Circles.

76. In no matters, including those agreed in this treaty and above all those concerning the Palatinate affair, shall any armed foreign power be tolerated to come onto German soil, unless it is with the grant, order and permission of the Emperor, and if this should occur then all effort shall be directed against it.

77. Furthermore, with the establishment and publication of this peace all unions, leagues, federations and suchlike agreements, as well as all oaths and duties sworn on the same, are totally null and void, and only the Imperial and Circle laws shall be kept, although this shall in no way imply any dissolution of the college of Electors.

Benecke (**13**), pp. 16–17.

document 8

The Treaty of Westphalia, 1648

Section A relates to the negotiations at Münster between the Emperor and France, and Section B to the negotiations at Osnabrück between Sweden, the Emperor and the Protestant German princes. Both were brought together and signed at Münster on 24 October 1648.

Section A

ARTICLE 1
There shall be a Christian, general and lasting peace, and true and genuine amity, between his sacred Imperial Majesty and his sacred Most Christian Majesty [the King of France]; as also between each

and all the allies and adherents of the said Imperial Majesty, the House of Austria, its heirs and successors, but chiefly the electors, princes and estates of the empire on the one hand; and each and all the allies and adherents of the said Most Christian Majesty, his heirs and successors, and primarily the most serene queen and the kingdom of Sweden, and the respective electors, princes and estates of the empire, on the other. And this peace shall be so honestly and earnestly preserved and cultivated that each party shall procure the advantage, honor and profit of the other, and that on all sides (both on the part of the whole Roman Empire as against the kingdom of France, and on the part of the kingdom of France towards the Roman Empire) true neighbourly relations shall be resumed and the care of peace and amity shall flourish again . . .

ARTICLE 62

But to prevent in future any differences arising in political matters, all and every the electors, princes and estates of the Roman Empire shall in this treaty be confirmed and secured in all their rights, prerogatives, liberties, privileges, in the free exercise of territorial rights both in ecclesiastical and in political matters, in their lordships and sovereign rights, and in the possession of all these; so that they never can or ought to be molested therein by anyone under any pretext whatsoever.

ARTICLE 63

They shall enjoy without contradiction the right of suffrage in all deliberations concerning the affairs of the empire, especially when the business in hand touches the making or interpreting of laws, the declaring of war, levying of taxes, raising or maintenance of troops, the erection on imperial behalf of new fortresses or the garrisoning of old in the territories of the states, also the conclusion of peace or of alliances, or similar matters. In these and like concerns nothing is in future to be done or admitted except by the common free choice and consent of all the imperial states. But particularly the individual states shall be for ever at liberty to enjoy the right of making alliances with each other and with other parties for their own support and security; always provided that such alliances shall not be directed against the emperor or empire, nor against the public peace of the empire, nor above all against the present treaty; and in everything without prejudice to the oath which everyone is bound to take to emperor and empire . . .

Section B

ARTICLE 5

Paragraph 1 ... The Religious Peace of 1555, as it was later confirmed ... by various imperial diets, shall, in all its articles entered into and concluded by the unanimous consent of the emperor, electors, princes and estates of both religions, be confirmed and observed fully and without infringement ... In all matters there shall be an exact and mutual equality between all the electors, princes and states of either religion, as far as agrees with the constitution of the realm, the imperial decrees, and the present treaty; so that what is right for one side shall also be right for the other; all violence and other contrary proceedings being herewith between the two sides for ever prohibited...

Paragraph 30. Whereas all immediate states enjoy, together with their territorial rights and sovereignty as hitherto used throughout the empire, also the right of reforming the practice of religion; and whereas in the Religious Peace the privilege of emigration was conceded to the subjects of such states if they dissented from the religion of their territorial lord; and whereas later, for the better preserving of greater concord among the states, it was agreed that no one should seduce another's subjects to his religion, or for that reason make any undertaking of defence or protection, or come to their aid for any reason; it is now agreed that all these be fully observed by the states of either religion, and that no state shall be hindered in the rights in matters of religion which belong to it by reason of its territorial independence and sovereignty...

ARTICLE 7

Paragraphs 1 and 2 ... It is agreed by the unanimous consent of His Imperial Majesty and all the estates of the empire that whatever rights and benefits are conferred upon the states and subjects attached to the Catholic and Augsburg faiths, either by the constitutions of the empire, or by the Religious Peace and this public treaty, ... shall also apply to those who are called reformed ... Beyond the religions mentioned above, none shall be received or tolerated in the Holy Empire...

G. Elton, Transl. from *Sammlung der Reichsabscheide*, ed. E. A. Koch, Frankfurt 1747, (**1**), p. 291–3.

The Papal Bull 'Zelo Domus Dei' (1648)

Reaction of Pope Innocent X to the treaty of Westphalia. The date given for the signing of the peace at Osnabrück (6 August, 1648) is not the one normally cited in modern accounts.

Consumed by zeal for the house of the Lord, we are especially concerned with the endeavour everywhere to maintain the integrity of the orthodox faith and the authority of the Catholic Church, so that the ecclesiastical rights of which we have been appointed guardian by our Saviour shall not in any way be impaired by those who seek their own interest rather than God's, and that we may not be accused of negligence when we shall render account to the Sovereign Judge. Accordingly it is not without deep pain that we have learned that by several articles in the peace concluded at Osnabrück, August 6, 1648, between our very dear son in Christ, Ferdinand, king of the Romans and emperor elect, his allies and adherents, on the one hand, and the Swedes, with their allies and adherents, on the other, as well as in that peace which was likewise concluded at Münster in Westphalia on the twenty-fourth day of October of this same year 1648, between the same Ferdinand, king of the Romans, etc., and our very dear son in Jesus Christ, Louis, the very Christian king of the French, his allies and adherents, great prejudice has been done to the Catholic religion, the divine service, the Roman apostolic see, the ecclesiastical order, their jurisdictions, authority, immunities, liberties exemptions, privileges, possessions, and rights; since by various articles in one of these treaties of peace the ecclesiastical possessions which the heretics formerly seized are abandoned to them and to their successors, and the heretics, called those of the Augsburg Confession, are permitted the free exercise of their heresy in various districts. They are promised places in which they may build temples for their worship and are admitted with the Catholics to public offices and positions...

The number seven of the electors of the empire, formerly ratified by the apostolic authority, is increased without our consent or that of the said see, and an eighth electorate has been erected in favor of Charles Louis, count of the Rhenish palatinate, a heretic. Many other things have been done too shameful to enumerate and very prejudicial to the orthodox religion and the Roman see...

[Accordingly] we assert and declare by these presents that all the said articles in one or both of the said treaties which in any way impair or prejudice in the slightest degree, or that can be said, alleged, understood, or imagined to be able in any way to injure or to have injured the Catholic religion, divine worship, the salvation of souls, the said Roman apostolic see, the inferior churches, the ecclesiastical order or estate, their persons, affairs, possessions, jurisdictions, authorities, immunities, liberties, privileges, prerogatives, and rights whatsoever, – all such provisions have been, and are of right, and shall perpetually be, null and void, invalid, iniquitous, unjust, condemned, rejected, frivolous, without force or effect, and no one is to observe them, even when they be ratified by oath..

Given at Rome in Santa Maria Maggiore, under seal of the fisherman's ring, November 26th of the year 1648, and of our pontificate the fifth.

J. H. Robinson (**10**), pp. 214–16.

document 10
The electoral convention at Regensburg, 1630

Here the electors discuss the complaints made against Wallenstein prior to his dismissal.

The electors, in a dignified and reasonable address, expressed their firm conviction that the whole blame for the misery, disgrace, and infamy, the cruel and unnecessary military exactions, which were daily increasing, rested with the new duke in Mechlenburg, who, as commander of the imperial forces, had been invested, without the consent of the estates, with such powers as no one before him had ever exercised. The soldiery, now become unspeakably numerous, served no other purpose than to lay waste the common fatherland. Moreover war has been waged upon those against whom it had never been declared. Contributions which, according to the decrees of the diet, no one had the right to demand without the consent of the assembled estates, were levied at the duke's own will and pleasure and wrung from the people in barbarous ways. It was shown that the electorate of Brandenburg alone in the last few years had furnished twenty million gulden, to say nothing of the terrible disturbances and destruction that war always brings with it. They complained, moreover, most bitterly of the excessive pomp and magnificence maintained by the duke and his officers, in the way of clothing, gold and silver utensils, and costly horses.

[Among the complaints from other princes and estates of the realm, the following, presented to the emperor by an ambassador from the duke of Pomerania, is especially noteworthy.] The duke of Pomerania doubts not that your Imperial Majesty has in remembrance how that he has at divers times protested against the unheard-of and unspeakable hardships and extortions which have now for almost three years been practised upon him and his subjects by the troops quartered in the land, and which still continue unabated; whereof he once more most earnestly complains, and humbly begs for relief. The burden has now become so great that he can bear it no longer.

According to the decisions and decrees of the imperial diet, he is under no obligation to support an army by himself and bear unaided a burden that should be divided among all the members of the empire. Nevertheless, for almost three years past, he has had to maintain within his dukedom and other territories over a hundred companies of your Imperial Majesty's army, besides sending supplies to outside points, and having the soldiery continually marching about the country. The outlay in the principality of Stettin alone amounts to fully ten million gulden; this can be verified at any time.

Worst of all are the vexatious means used in collecting these monthly contributions from our officials and subjects. A new and unheard-of *modus extorquendi* has been invented, such as was never before practised by honest soldiers quartered in a friendly land; and the exactions are carried out with such rigorous excess under the officers in charge that the miserable victims can scarce keep shirts on their backs. And what insolent excesses and wilful interference with church services, despoiling of churches, violation of graves of the dead, infringements of every sort of our sovereignty and authority, disarming of our subjects and curtailing of our revenue as ruler! This last has actually gone so far that it is impossible for us, from all the length and breadth of our land, to maintain a table befitting our princely rank; whereas every captain, out of his own district alone, lives in more than princely style and sends away large sums besides. Toward the poor people they are barbarous and tyrannical beyond words, beating, burning, and plundering, and depriving them of the very necessities of existence, till they are in danger of soul as well as body, for they are driven to

such unnatural and inhuman food as buds of trees and grass, and
even to the flesh of their own children and of dead bodies.

Robinson (**10**), pp. 205–7.

document 11

A modern historian on Wallenstein

There were three Wallensteins. First the man of flesh and blood,
with the sombre groundwork of his soul, his harshness and greed,
his secretiveness and his copious candour, his dreams and his
sufferings. Lastly the image of him fashioned for themselves by his
enemies, with exacerbated suspicions and clumsy determination of
the indeterminable. 'The common, false repute of this lord', Bavarian Field-Marshall von Pappenheim wrote to Maximilian, 'is so
imbued into folk that I can oft only with difficulty prevent myself
from believing all tidings of the like as are so circumstantially told
of him, although I was by him at the very time and hour as that
which is narrated as happening'. And then, between these poles,
was something else, something intermediate, an aura around the
real person in whose creation his enemies participated and he too.
After all, not every leader of his day was execrated, exalted and
interminably discussed in this way. That was his fate, not that of
his rivals. He provoked it without always being true to the aura.

G. Mann (**55**), p. 400.

document 12

Gustavus Adolphus' reaction to his luke-warm reception by the German princes after his invasion.

*Here he argues with the ambassador from his brother-in-law, the Elector of
Brandenburg (July 1630).*

I have received your explanation of the grounds on which my
honoured brother-in-law seeks to dissuade me from this war. I
confess I should have expected a different sort of embassy, since
God has brought me thus far, and since I have come into this land
for no other purpose than to free it from the thieves and robbers
who have so plagued it, and, first and foremost, to help his
Excellency out of his difficulties. Does his Excellency then not

know that the emperor and his followers do not mean to rest till the evangelical religion is wholly rooted out of the empire, and that his Excellency has nothing else to expect than being forced either to deny his religion or to leave his country? Does he think by prayers and beseechings and such like means to obtain something different?

For God's sake, bethink yourselves and take counsel like men! I cannot go back – *jacta est alea: transivimus Rubiconem.* I seek not my own advantage in this war, nor any gain save the security of my kingdom; I can look for nothing but expense, hard work, trouble, and danger to life and limb. I have found reason enough for my coming in that Prussia has twice sent aid to my enemies and attempted to overthrow me; thereafter they tried to seize the east port, which made it plain enough what designs they had against me. Even so has his Excellency, the elector, like reasons, and the time has come for him to open his eyes and face the situation, instead of acting as the representative – nay, rather servant – of the emperor in his own land; *qui se fait brebis, le loup le mange.*

Now is his opportunity, since his territory is free of the emperor's troops, to garrison and defend his fortresses. If he will not do this, let him give me a single stronghold, – Custrin, for instance, – and I will defend it, and you can persist in the indolence that your master loves. What other course is there open? For I tell you plainly that I will know nor hear nothing of 'neutrality'; his Excellency must be either friend or foe. When I reach his frontier he must declare himself either hot or cold. The fight is between God and the devil. If his Excellency is on God's side, let him stand by me; if he holds rather with the devil, then he must fight with me; there is no third course, – that is certain.

Robinson (**10**), pp. 209–11.

The sack of Magdeburg, May 1631

document 13

So then General Pappenheim collected a number of his people on the ramparts by the New Town, and brought them from there into the streets of the city. Von Falckenberg was shot, and fires were kindled in different quarters; then indeed it was all over with the city, and further resistance was useless. Nevertheless some of the soldiers and citizens did try to make a stand here and there, but the imperial troops kept bringing on more and more forces – cavalry, too – to help them, and finally they got the Kröckenthor open and let in the whole imperial army and the forces of the Catholic League, – Hungarians, Croats, Poles, Walloons, Italians, Spaniards, French, North and South Germans.

Thus it came about that the city and all its inhabitants fell into the hands of the enemy, whose violence and cruelty were due in part to their common hatred of the adherents of the Augsburg Confession, and in part to their being imbittered by the chain shot which had been fired at them and by the derision and insults that the Magdeburgers had heaped upon them from the ramparts.

Then was there naught but beating and burning, plundering, torture, and murder. Most especially was every one of the enemy bent on securing much booty. When a marauding party entered a house, if its master had anything to give he might thereby purchase respite and protection for himself and his family till the next man, who also wanted something, should come along. It was only when everything had been brought forth and there was nothing left to give that the real trouble commenced. Then, what with blows and threats of shooting, stabbing, and hanging, the poor people were so terrified that if they had had anything left they would have brought it forth if it had been buried in the earth or hidden away in a thousand castles. In this frenzied rage, the great and splendid city that had stood like a fair princess in the land was now, in its hour of direst need and unutterable distress and woe, given over to the flames, and thousands of innocent men, women, and children, in the midst of a horrible din of heartrending shrieks and cries, were tortured and put to death in so cruel and shameful a manner that no words would suffice to describe, nor no tears to bewail it ...

Thus in a single day this noble and famous city, the pride of the whole country, went up in fire and smoke; and the remnant of its citizens, with their wives and children, were taken prisoners and driven away by the enemy with a noise of weeping and wailing that could be heard from afar, while the cinders and ashes from the town were carried by the wind to Wanzleben, Egeln, and still more distant places ...

In addition to all this, quantities of sumptuous and irreplaceable house furnishings and movable property of all kinds, such as books, manuscripts, paintings, memorials of all sorts, ... which money could not buy, were either burned or carried away by the soldiers as booty. The most magnificent garments, hangings, silk stuffs, gold and silver lace, linen of all sorts, and other household goods were bought by the army sutlers for a mere song and peddled about by the cart load all through the archbishopric of Magdeburg

111

and in Anhalt and Brunswick. Gold chains and rings, jewels, and every kind of gold and silver utensils were to be bought from the common soldiers for a tenth of their real value ...

Robinson (**10**), pp. 211–12

document 14
Peasant reaction to the Swedish army near Swabia, 1632

As reported to the London press.

The whole bishopric of Freisingen is freely yielded up to His Majesty and paid him contribution. Hereupon some boors in Swaben being 10,000 strong have assembled themselves together, they have taken again Leutkirch and Wangen, they have with them some pieces of ordnance. But some of our forces which are already sent against them will soon cool their courage.

This week the afore mentioned boors did overcome and surprise fifty Swedish soldiers between Schrobenhousen and Sticha, [and] did cut off their ears and noses, chopped off their hands and feet, and put out their eyes, and so left them, these devilish boors do great mischief of the like nature.

As soon as the king of Sweden was advertised of the cruell insolencies of these boors he was much displeased, and so much more because he saw that his soldiers would not put it up but presently cried revenge and fired their villages, insomuch that in one day there were seen 200 several fires blazing at once.

The Swedish Intelligencer (**12**)

document 15
More effects of the war on Germany

Here superintendent Andrea describes the effects on Calw in Württemberg.

Through murder, plunder, beating and burning, taking of people and other destructive activities, we have been reduced to one third of our population. We were 3,832 and we have lost 2,304, leaving only 1,528 of us. Those of us who remain would consider ourselves fortunate if only, as is granted to various other destroyed places, we were left alone to assess our own losses which are in excess of a ton of gold, but instead we are further burdened so that our ruinous condition will finally exhaust and flatten us. The number of destitute is so large that they run to 500 or 600 head and in our town treasury there is not one farthing left. From among the citizens alone there are 125 persons in the hospital and even more still in their houses who have to be supplied regularly. It is not possible to say how much this relief costs us, since even the richest can hardly supply their own families with necessities.

Yet we would perhaps have been able to bear these costs since Christian love always finds a way with charity, if only the fierce war tax paid to ward off plundering [*Brandschatzung*] for a third time had not sucked us dry. Our poor town had to pay 800 gulden *per week* over and above the fixed rate. It was collected with extreme severity and it came on top of all our existing worries, especially since plague and hunger claim 100 to 150 victims monthly from among our ranks, so that those who remain alive also have to pay the tax assessments of the dead.

However, this was not the sum total of our plight. You know that all our livelihood consisted of weaving and dyeing of cloth, and if we lost or were prevented from carrying out these activities, then a knife would really be at our throats, since we depend on this work. With all the destruction and shrinkage of population we still have 243 master craftsmen in this profession. Yet they have no employment, to their great vexation. Added to them are another 64 from the immediate neighbourhood, who, like us, are out of work. But the gloom still does not end there. As the fable says, when the stomach is denied nourishment, all the members suffer, so one can say about Calw that when this [textile manufacture] is blocked, the whole neighbourhood must bleed to death. In the vicinity there are 1,200 textile workers who depend on the town for contracts, as well as a similar amount or even more women spinners, as I know for certain from the registers. When Calw starves, most of the region around it starves too ...

Beneke (**13**), p. 37.

Conditions in 1634

The curé of Emael (in the Basse-Meuse) in this diary entry describes the effect of sickness, famine, fire and war (1634).

This year, we have been tested in an astonishing fashion by sickness, war, famine, and fire. First, a violent plague struck the village during the months of June and July, taking seventeen victims. Immediately afterwards, war unexpectedly came to us. The army of the King of Spain commanded by the Marquis of Aytona constructed a fort at Navagne, near the Meuse. Then, when it appeared they were going to put siege to Maastricht, they camped, some at Montenaken, others at Lanacken, and a large part of the army here at Emael. The Marquis of Salada lodged here with three legions or regiments, one of infantry and two of cavalry. They behaved worse than barbarously; they destroyed everything; they cut trees, completely demolished many houses, and trampled whatever grain they could not steal, not even leaving enough to appease the hunger of the poor farmers. For that reason, we did not collect the tithe this year.

My house situated beside the cemetery, suffered an equally terrible destruction. I, Antoine Henrice, curé of Emael, had hardly recovered from the contagious malady that had struck me a short time before. I was not even able to leave the house without exposing myself to great danger, nor flee the impertinent Spanish soldiers as I would have wished. They hunted everywhere for food, straw, and other materials in order to construct their barracks. I was belatedly aided by one of their chaplains; together we chased them away as best we could. I offered lodging in my house to some soldiers, but it was in vain: they were afraid they would catch my illness. In the end, several who were more adventuresome did so, bringing their horses and coming to stay in my house, which they treated like their own and preserved from harm.

I began my sickness on 20 July; the Spanish arrived at Emael on 2 August and retired on 8 September, the feast of the birth of the Holy Virgin, which fell on a Friday.

Edm. van Wintershoven, *Cronique tirée des registres paroisiaux d' Emael*, BSSL. 22 (1904), 58–59, in Eutmann (**106**), p. 196.

document 17
Peasants are forced to flee to Lake Constance (1636)

The imperial soldiers are staying there and committing all sorts of villainy and so the subjects dare not live there, nor remain in the villages. And so from all the surrounding villages – Mimmenhaussen, Neyffra, Weilldorf and Düffingen – all the subjects have moved into the monastery here. with wife and child, all their goods, cattle, horses, pigs and everything they had, so that the courtyard, the hospital, the eating rooms, women's house, the stonemason's house ... barns ... stable and stalls, the gatekeeper's lodge, in other words, all the places were completely full through the whole horribly cold winter (in which many froze ...) and summer until the autumn.

S. Bürster, *Beschreibung des schwedischen Krieges, 1630–47*, F. von Weech, ed. Leipzig, 1875, p. 98.

document 18
The pressure of Spanish economic warfare in the 1620s backfires.

From Cavsas por donde crecio alcomercio de Olanda y se hizo un monopolio universal

With the *almirantazgo* all the trade of the entire world passed to Holland and Amsterdam ... for the *almirantazgo*, armed with the decrees against contraband, especially that of 15 October 1625, closed the door to all commerce, of friends and enemies alike, with their certificates, inspections, condemnations and confiscations such that within a short time, Spain was without trade, ships, supplies or foodstuffs, customs revenues fell and the produce of the country was without means of exit.

Brit. Lib. Add. Ms, 14005 fo. 27 cited in Israel (**111**), p. 51.

document 19
Swedish state income and expenditure in 1633
In *riksdaler*

Income	*1633*
Sweden and Finland	
'Ordinary' revenue	1,229,920
'Extraordinary' revenue	573,872
Customs and excise	22,040
Loans	59,384
French subsidies	400,000
Estonia, Livonia, Ingria	
Ship tolls and customs	125,299
Other income	238,937
Prussian ship tolls	614,000
Total	**3,263,452**

Expenditure

Sweden and Finland	
Court expenses	15,753
Salaries of council of state	55,752
Judicial salaries	3,059
Chancery and foreign affairs	5,233
Exchequer and financial administration	1,351
Army and army administration	358,524
Navy and naval administration	84,202
Local government	96,769
Debts paid	107,123
Other expenses	350,882
Estonia, Livonia, Ingria	304,462
	1,473,120
Deductions from revenue	753,789
Total expenditure	**2,226,909**
Total income	**3,263,452**
Surplus	**1,036,543**

Taken from Astrom (**71**), pp. 82–83.

document 20

French diplomatic thinking

(i)   *Richelieu in 1629*

France's only thought must be to strengthen herself and to open doors so that she may enter the states of all her neighbours to protect them from Spain's oppression when the opportunities to do so arise ... We must look to the fortification of Metz and advance as far as Strassburg if this is possible, to acquire an entry to Germany .. [though] this must be done in the fulness of time, with great discretion and by unobtrusive secret negotiation.

Pagès (**31**)., p. 118.

(ii)   *Richelieu in 1632*

It is more difficult to recognise the illness than to cure it, all the more so because of the very violence of the illness. Moreover, in this case the old maxim of meeting force with force cannot apply, since to do so would put France and Christendom in extreme danger, for reasons which are well known to men of sound judgement and who can apply in matters of statesmanship the same care as doctors who avoid drastic purges during prolonged fevers. The chief difficulty lies in the contradiction presented by the disease, for we are torn between fear of the house of Austria and fear of the Protestants. The perfect answer would be to reduce both to such a point that they are no longer to be feared, and it is to this end that efforts must be directed. But at the same time care must be taken to ensure that if the means used do not attain this end, the perfect answer, they should at least serve to ward off the worst effects and provide breathing space in which to muster one's forces and turn events to account without danger ... As to the Spaniard and the Swede, we must above all take care that in bringing down one we do not raise the other to such a point that he is more to be feared than the former. We must also act with such caution that instead of setting one against the other, we do not become involved in war with one of them. Such a step would allow the other to increase in such strength that even if the king were victorious he would lose more from the easy manner in which the other became more powerful than he would gain from his own victory ... To carry out this difficult operation, in which the issues are so delicate, we must combine industry with force, and diplomacy with arms.

Pagès (**31**), pp. 139–40.

(iii) *A Spanish envoy at Westphalia reporting a conversation with a French envoy, D'Avaux, on inter-state attitudes.*

He confessed to me that they had a profound apprehension of the power of the Austrian dynasty, seeing Spain and the Empire acting in conjunction. I replied that of course the princes of the House of Habsburg had a close accord, being cousins and friends, but neither had nurtured designs against the interests of France. The proper fear that France should have was of the power of the Church's enemies, which threatened all three crowns, which should therefore unite and not destroy each other.

Stradling (**201**), p. 106.

(iv) *Cardinal Mazarin on the Treaty of Westphalia from a letter to the French envoy, Servien, October 1648.*

It might perhaps have been more useful for achieving a general peace if the war could have been pursued a little longer in Germany, instead of our haste to find an accommodation as we have now done. Yet this would have implied that we were in a position to prolong negotiations when instead there was the threat that Sweden might have betrayed us and acted on her own urgent desire to conclude hostilities. The fear of such an unpleasant event overrode all other considerations. I think that the fear of total collapse by the Emperor which, considering his pathetic situation was unavoidably imminent, may have been enough to invite sympathy from the Spaniards, cause them somewhat to soften their harsh stand, and protect him from such a blow. Whereas now they consider him to be secured by the conclusion of peace, despite the conditions, which are quite harsh to him, and they take no more notice of him, nor do they seem to worry about his position, which may otherwise have been a more serious reason for bringing them to conclude peace ...

Furthermore, I gather from a reliable source that the Emperor ... has assured the king of Spain ... that this peace is certainly damaging in its hard terms, but that given the situation under which it was concluded, it is very advantageous. A great number of fortified places and lands have been returned to him, which he had already lost, giving him the opportunity to save the rest, which under other circumstances would have been subject to the greatest danger. Since he has now deflected such a powerful blow and has got his breath back somewhat, he is ready at any time to take up the war again, whenever he chooses. For this there would certainly be no lack of pretext, if only he could find the necessary means for his disposal.

L. Bäte, *Der Freide in Osnabrück*, Oldenburg, 1948, p. 147, transl. in G. Benecke, *Germany in the Thirty Years War*, Arnold, 1978, pp. 18–19.

Bibliography

DOCUMENTS AND CONTEMPORARY ACCOUNTS

1 Elton, G. R. (ed.), *Renaissance and Reformation 1300–1648*, Collier–Macmillan, 1968.
2 The *Fugger Newsletters*, London, 1924.
3 Gardiner, S. R. (ed.), *Letters and Correspondence England–Germany 1618–20*, 2 vols Camden Society, London, 1865/8.
4 Grimmelshausen, H. J. C. von., *Simplicius Simplicissimus*, translated by H. Weissenborn & L. Macdonald, John Calder, 1964.
5 Hollaender, A., 'Some English Documents on the End of Wallenstein', in *Bulletin of the John Rylands Library*, XL, 1958.
6 Macartney, C. A. (ed.), *The Habsburg and Hohenzollern Dynasties in the 17th and 18th Centuries*, (Documentary History of Western Civilisation), Macmillan, 1970.
7 Monro, R., *Monro his expedition with the worthy Scots regiment called Mackay's*, London, 1637.
8 Reich, E. (ed.), *Select Documents Illustrating Medieval and Modern History*, King & Son, 1905.
9 Roberts, M. (ed.), *Sweden as a Great Power 1611–97*, Arnold, 1968.
10 Robinson, J. H., *Readings in European History*, vol. 2, Ginn & Co., 1906.
11 Schulz, H., (ed.), *Der dreissigjährige Kreig*, Leipzig, 1917.
12 *The Swedish Intelligencer*, Cambridge University Library. Acton d. sel 601, 2, 3.

GENERAL

13 Benecke, G., *Germany in the Thirty Years War*, Arnold, 1978.
14 Briggs, R., *Early Modern France 1560–1715*, Oxford University Press, 1977.
15 Clark, G. N., *The Seventeenth Century*, Oxford University Press, 1947.
16 Cooper, J. (ed.), *The New Cambridge Modern History IV: The Decline of Spain and the Thirty Years War 1609–48/59*, Cambridge University Press, 1970.
17 Elliott, J. H., *Imperial Spain 1469–1719*, Penguin, 1970.

18 Elliott, J. H., *Europe Divided 1559–98*, Fontana, 1968.

19 Evans, R. J. W., *Rudolf II and His World*, Oxford University Press, 1973.

20 Gindely, A., *History of the Thirty Years War*, 2 vol, London 1885.

21 Hughes, M. and Kamen, H., 'The Thirty Years War', in *European History 1500–1700*, Sussex Books, 1976.

22 Koenigsberger, H. G., *The Habsburgs and Europe 1516–1660*, Cornell University Press, 1971.

23 Langer, H., *The Thirty Years War*, Blandford, 1980.

24 Lisk, J., *The Struggle for Supremacy in the Baltic 1600–1725*, (London History Studies), Hodder & Stoughton, 1968.

25 Livet, G., *La guerre de trente ans*, Paris, 1963.

26 Maland, D., *Europe at War 1600–50*, Macmillan, 1980.

27 McNeill, W. H., *Europe's Steppe Frontier 1500–1800*, University of Chicago Press, 1964.

28 Ogg, D., *Europe in the Seventeenth Century*, A. & C. Black, 1971.

29 Parker, G., *Europe in Crisis 1598–1648*, Fontana, 1979.

30 Parker, G. (ed.), *The Thirty Years War*, Routledge & Kegan Paul, 1984.

31 Pagès, G., *The Thirty Years War 1618–48*, A. & C. Black, 1970.

32 Polisensky, J. V., 'The Thirty Years War', in *Past and Present*, no. 6, 1954.

33 Polisensky, J. V., *The Thirty Years War*, Batsford, 1971.

34 Polisensky, J. V., *War and Society in Europe 1618–48*, Cambridge University Press, 1978.

35 Rabb, T. K, (ed.), *The Thirty Years War*, D. C. Heath, 1972.

36 Rabb, T. K., *The Struggle for Stability in Early Modern Europe*, Oxford University Press, 1975.

37 Reade, H. G. R., *Sidelights on the Thirty Years War*, 3 vols. London, 1924.

38 Schiller, F., *The History of the Thirty Years War*, London, 1901.

39 Shennan, J. H., *The Origins of the Modern European State 1450–1725*, Hutchinson Educational. 1974.

40 Steinberg, S. H., *The Thirty Years War and the Conflict for European Hegemony 1600–60*, Arnold, 1966.

41 Wedgwood, C. V., *The Thirty Years War*, Cape, 1938.

MILITARY

42 Alcalá–Zamora, J., *España, Flanders, y el Mar del Norte 1618–39*, Barcelona, 1975.

43 Beller, E. A., 'The Military Expedition of Sir Charles

Morgan to Germany 1627–9', in *English Historical Review*, vol. XLIII, 1928, pp, 528–39.

44 Bog, I., *Die bäuerliche Wirtschaft im Zeitalter des Dreissigjährigen Krieges*, Coburg, 1952.

45 Corvisier, A., *Armées et Sociétés en Europe de 1494 à 1789*, Paris, 1976.

46 Diwald, H., *Wallenstein, Eine Biographie*, Ullstein paperback, 1975.

47 Duffy, C., *Siege Warfare: The Fortress in the Early Modern World 1494–1660*, Routledge & Kegan Paul, 1979.

48 Duffy, M. (ed.), *The Military Revolution and the State 1500–1800*, (Exeter Studies in History, 1), University of Exeter, 1980.

49 Eggenberger, D., *A Dictionary of Battles*, Allen & Unwin, 1968.

50 Field, M., 'Middle Class Society and the Rise of Military Professionalism: The Dutch Army 1589–1609', in *Armed Forces and Society* (1), August 1975.

51 Hale, J. R., 'The Early Development of the Bastion: an Italian Chronology c1450–c1534', in *Europe and the later Middle Ages*, ed. J. R. Hale, J., Highfield, and B. Smalley, Faber, 1965.

52 Hall, A. R., *Ballistics in the seventeenth Century. A Study in the Relations of Science and War with reference to England*, Cambridge University Press, 1952.

53 Howard, M., *War in European History*, Oxford University Press, 1976.

54 Mallett, M. E., *Mercenaries and their Masters: Warfare in Renaissance Italy*, Bodley Head, 1974.

55 Mann, G., *Wallenstein. His Life Narrated*, Deutsch, 1976.

56 Oman, C., *A History of the Art of War in the 16th Century*, London, 1937.

57 Parker, G., *The Army of Flanders and the Spanish Road 1567–1659*, Cambridge University Press, 1972.

58 Parker, G., 'The Military Revolution – a Myth?', in *Journal of Modern History*, vol. XLVIII, 1976.

59 Redlich, F., *De Praeda Militari: Looting and Booty*, Wiesbaden, 1956.

60 Redlich, F., 'Contributions in the Thirty Years War', in *Economic History Review*, 2nd Series, 12, 1959–60.

61 Redlich, F., *The German Military Enterpriser and his workforce. A Study in European Economic and Social History*, 2 vols, Wiesbaden, 1964–5.

62 Roberts, M., 'The Military Revolution 1560–1660', in M. Roberts, (ed.), *Essays in Swedish History*, Weidenfeld & Nicolson, 1967.

63 Rothenburg, G. E., *The Austrian Military Border in Croatia 1522–1747*, Urbana, 1960.

64 Taylor, H., 'Trade, Neutrality, and the English Road 1630–48', in *Economic History Review*, 2nd Series, 25, 1972.

65 Thompson, I. A. A., *War and Government in Habsburg Spain, 1560–1620*, Athlone Press, 1976.

66 Schiller, F., *Wallenstein*, D. C. Heath, 1902.

67 Van Creveld, M., *Supplying War. Logistics from Wallenstein to Patton*, Cambridge University Press, 1977.

68 Wagner, E., *European Weapons and Warfare 1618–48*, Octopus Books, 1979.

69 Watson, F., *Wallenstein: Soldier under Saturn*, Chatto & Windus, 1938.

ECONOMIC AND SOCIAL

70 Aston, T. (ed.), *Crisis in Europe 1560–1660*, [Essays from Past and Present], Routledge & Kegan Paul, 1965.

71 Aström, S–E, 'The Swedish Economy and Sweden's Role as a Great Power 1632–97', in M. Roberts, (ed.), *Sweden's Age of Greatness 1632–1718*, Macmillan, 1973.

72 Baehrel, R., *Une croissance: La Basse Provence rurale*, Paris, 1961.

73 Barbour, V., *Capitalism in Amsterdam in the Seventeenth Century*, AMS Press, 1963.

74 Beller, E. A., *Propaganda in Germany in the Thirty Years War*, Princeton, 1940.

75 Benecke, G., 'The Problem of Death and Destruction in Germany during the Thirty Years War: New Evidence from the Middle Weser Front', in *European Studies Review*, 1972.

76 Benecke, G., 'Labour Relations and Peasant Society in North–West Germany c. 1600', in *History*, vol. 58, 1973.

77 Benecke, G., *Society and Politics in Germany 1500–1750*, Routledge & Kegan Paul, 1974.

78 Benecke, G., 'The Westphalian Circle and the County of Lippe and Imperial Currency Control' in J. A. Vann and S.W. Rowan (eds.), *The Old Reich*, Brussels, 1974.

79 Bogucka, M., 'Amsterdam and the Baltic in the First Half of the Seventeenth Century', in *Economic History Review*, 2nd Series, 26, 1973.

80   Bonney, R.J., 'The Secret Expenses of Richelieu and Mazarin, 1624–62', in *English Historical Review*, 361, 1976.

81   Bonney, R.J., *The King's Debts: Finance and Politics in France 1589–1661*, Oxford University Press, 1982.

82   Bowman, F.J., 'Dutch Diplomacy and the Baltic Grain Trade 1600–60', in *Pacific Historical Review*, V, 1936.

83   Boxer, C.R., *The Dutch Seaborne Empire*, Hutchinson Educational, 1977.

84   Boxer, C.R., *The Portuguese Seaborne Empire, 1415–1825*, Hutchinson Educational, 1977.

85   Braudel, F., *The Mediterranean and the Mediterranean World in the Age of Philip II*, 2 vols, Fontana, 1975.

86   Chaunu, H. and P., *Séville et l'Atlantique, 1504–1650*, Paris, 1955–60, vol. VIII [although see essay in P. Earle, (**95**)].

87   Christensen, A.E., *Dutch Trade to the Baltic about 1600*, Copenhagen, 1941.

88   Chuboda, B., *Spain and the Empire, 1519–1643*, Chicago, 1952.

89   Cippolla, C., 'The Decline of Italy', in *Economic History Review*, 5, 1952.

90   Cipolla, C, (ed.), *The Sixteenth and Seventeenth Centuries*, Fontana Economic History, 1974.

91   Cipolla, C., *Before the Industrial Revolution: European Society and Economy, 1000–1700*, Methuen, 1981.

92   Collins, J.B., 'Sur l'histoire fiscale du XVII siècle: les impôts directs en Champagne entre 1595 et 1635', in *Annales E.S.C.* xxxiv, 1979, pp. 325–47.

93   Coveney, P.J, (ed.), *France in Crisis 1620–75*, Rowman & Littlefield, 1977.

94   Dillen, J.G. van, 'Amsterdam's Role in Seventeenth Century Dutch Politics and its Economic Background', in J.S. Bromley and E.H. Kossmann (eds.), *Britain and the Netherlands*, vol. 2, Gröningen, 1964.

95   Earle, P. (ed.), *Essays in European Economic History, 1500–1800*, Oxford University Press, 1974.

96   Eddy, J., 'The "Maunder Minimum": Sunspots and Climate in the Reign of Louis XIV', in G. Parker and L. Smith

97   Edmundson, G., *Anglo–Dutch Rivalry*, Oxford, 1911.

98   Elliott, J.H., *The Revolt of the Catalans*, Cambridge University Press, 1963.

99   Elliott, J.H., 'Revolution and Continuity', in G. Parker and L. Smith (eds.), *op cit*, (**132** ch. 5).

100   Evans, R.J.W., *The Making of the Habsburg Monarchy*

1550–1700, Oxford University Press, 1979.

101 Franz, G., *Der Dreissigjährije Kreig und das Deutsche Volk*, 3rd edn, Stuttgart, 1960.

102 Freytag, G., *Pictures of German Life*, London, 1862.

103 Friedrichs, C. R., *Urban Society in an Age of War: Nördlingen, 1580–1720*, Princeton University Press, 1979.

104 Goubert, P., *Beauvais et le Beauvasis de 1600 à 1730*, Paris, 1960, [though see the abridged version *Cent Mille Provinciaux au XVII siècle: Beauvais et le Beauvasis de 1600 à 1730*, Paris, 1968].

105 Greene, J. P. and Forster, R., *Preconditions of Revolution in Early Modern Europe*, Baltimore, 1970.

106 Gutman, M., *War and Rural Life in the Early Modern Low Countries*, Princeton University Press, 1980.

107 Hamilton, E. J., *American Treasure and the Price Revolution in Spain, 1501–1650*, Cambridge, Mass., 1934.

108 Hoboken, W. J. van, 'The Dutch West India Company: the Political Background of its Rise and Decline' in J. S. Bromley and E. H. Kossmann (eds.), *Britain and the Netherlands*, vol. 1, Chatto & Windus, 1960.

109 Hobsbawm, E. J., 'The Overall Crisis of the European Economy in the Seventeenth Century', in *Past and Present*, no 5, 1954, pp. 33–53.

110 Hopkins, S. V., and Phelps Brown, E. H., 'Seven Centuries of the Prices of Consumables, compared with Builders Wage Rates', in *Economica*, 23, 1956.

111 Israel, J. I., 'A Conflict of Empires: Spain and the Netherlands 1618–48', in *Past and Present*, no 76, 1977, pp. 34–74.

112 Israel, J. I., *The Dutch Republic and the Hispanic World, 1606–61*, Oxford University Press, 1982.

113 Johnson, C., *Revolutionary Change*, Boston, 1966.

114 Judges, A. V., *Philip Burlamachi: a Financier of the Thirty Years War*, Princeton, 1940.

115 Kamen, H., 'The Economic and Social Consequences of the Thirty Years War', in *Past and Present*, no. 39, 1968.

116 Kamen, H., *The Iron Century: Social Change in Europe 1550–1660*, Cardinal, 1976.

117 Kellenbenz, H., 'Germany', in C. Wilson and G. Parker (eds.), *An Introduction to the Sources of European Economic History, 1500–1800*, Methuen, 1980.

118 Kellenbenz, H., *The Rise of the European Economy*, revised edn, G. Benecke, Weidenfeld & Nicolson, 1976.

119 Kepler, J. S., 'Fiscal Aspects of the English Carrying Trade

during the Thirty Years War', in *Economic History Review*, 25, 1972.

120 Kierstead, R. F. (ed.), *State and Society in Seventeenth Century France*, New York, 1975.

121 Klimá, A., 'Industrial Development in Bohemia after the Thirty Years War', in *Past and Present*, no. 11, 1957.

122 Lammert, G., *Geschichte der Seuchen. Hungers-und Kriegsnoth zur Zeit des Dreissigjährigen Kreiges*, New printing, Wiesbaden, 1971.

123 Le Roy Ladurie, E., *Les Paysans de Languedoc*, Paris, 1966, English translation by J. Day, University of Illinois Press, 1977.

124 Lossky, A., 'The General European Crisis of the 1680s', in *European Studies Review*, no. 2, April 1980.

125 Ludloff, R., 'Industrial Development in Sixteenth- and Seventeenth-Century Germany', in *Past and Present*, no. 12, 1957.

126 Merriman, R. B., *Six Contemporaneous Revolutions*, Oxford, 1938.

127 Moote, A. L., 'The Preconditions of Revolutions in Early Modern Europe: Did they really exist?', in G. Parker and L. Smith, *op cit* (**132**).

128 Nef, J. U., *The Rise of the British Coal Industry*, F. Cass, 1966.

129 Nef, J. U., *Western Civilization since the Renaissance*, Harper Torch, 1963.

130 Neveaux, H., Jacquart, J. and Le Roy Ladurie, E. (eds.), *Histoire de la France Rurale*, vol. 2, Paris, 1975.

131 Ortiz, A. D., *La Sociedad Española en el siglo XVII*, 2 vols., Madrid, 1963–69.

132 Parker, G. and Smith, L. (eds.), *The General Crisis of the Seventeenth Century*, Routledge & Kegan Paul, 1978.

133 Polisensky, J. V., 'The Thirty Years War and the Crises and Revolutions of Seventeenth Century Europe', in *Past and Present*, no. 39, 1968.

134 Rabb, T. K., 'The Effects of the Thirty Years War on the German Economy', in *Journal of Modern History*, no 24, 1962.

135 Rich, E. E. and Wilson, C. H., *The Cambridge Economic History of Europe*, vols. IV and V, Cambridge University Press, 1967 & 1977.

136 Richardson, R. C., *The Debate on the English Revolution*, Methuen, 1977.

137 Roberts, M., 'Queen Christina and the General Crisis of the

Seventeenth Century' in *Past and Present*, no. 22, 1962.

138 Romano, R., 'Between the Sixteenth and Seventeenth Centuries: the Economic Crisis of 1619–22', in G. Parker and L. Smith, (eds.), *op. cit.* (**132**).

139 Sagarra, I. E., *A Social History of Germany 1648–1914*, Methuen, 1977.

140 Salmon, J. H. M., 'Venality of Office and Popular Sedition in Seventeenth Century France: A Review of a Controversy', in *Past and Present*, no. 37, 1967.

141 Schöffer, I., 'Did Holland's Golden Age Coincide with a Period of Crisis?', in G. Parker and L. Smith, *op. cit.* (**132**).

142 Sella, D., in B. Pullen, (ed.), *Crisis and Change in the Venetian Economy*, London, 1968.

143 Slicher van Bath, B. H., *Yield Ratios 1810–1820*, A.A.G. Bijdragen, vol. 9, 1963.

144 Slicher van Bath, B. H., *The Agrarian History of Western Europe*, London, 1963.

145 Spooner, F. C., *The International Economy and Monetary Movements in France, 1493–1725*, Harvard University Press, 1972.

146 Spooner, F. C., 'The European Economy 1609–50', in J. P. Cooper (ed.), *New Cambridge Modern History*, vol. IV, Cambridge University Press, 1970.

147 Steensgaard, N., 'The Seventeenth-Century Crisis', in G. Parker and L. Smith, *op. cit.* (**132**).

148 Stone, L., *The Causes of the English Revolution, 1529–1642*, Routledge & Kegan Paul, 1972.

149 Stradling, R. A., 'Seventeenth Century Spain: Decline or Survival?', in *European Studies Review*, vol. 9, 1979.

150 Vives, J. V., *An Economic History of Spain*, London, 1969.

151 Vries, J. de, *The Economy of Europe in an Age of Crisis, 1600–1750*, Cambridge University Press, 1976.

152 Wilson, C. H. and Parker, G. (eds.), *An Introduction to the Sources of European Economic History 1500–1800*, Methuen, 1978.

153 Zagorin, P., *Rebels and Rulers, 1500–1660*, 2 vols., Cambridge University Press, 1982.

RELIGION AND DIPLOMACY

154 Adams, S. L., 'Foreign Policy and the Parliaments of 1621 and 1624', in K. M. Sharpe, (ed.), *Faction and Parliament*, Oxford University Press, 1978.

155 Albrecht, D., *Richelieu, Gustav Adolf und das Reich*, Munich, 1959.

156 Albrecht, D., *Die Aswärtige Politik Maximilians von Bayern 1618–35*, Göttingen, 1962.

157 Batten, J. M., 'Political Factors in Movements toward Christian Unity in Seventeenth Century Europe', in *Church History*, 1943.

158 Bierther, K., *Der Regensburger Reichstag von 1640–1664*, Kallmünz, 1971.

159 Bireley, R., 'The Peace of Prague (1635) and the Counter–Reformation in Germany', in *Journal of Modern History*, XLVII, 1976.

160 Bireley, R., *Religion and Politics in the Age of Counter–Reformation: Emperor Ferdinand II, William Lamormaini, SJ, and the Formation of Imperial Policy*, University of North Carolina Press, London, 1982.

161 Bonney, R. J., *Political Change in France under Richelieu and Mazarin, 1624–66*, Oxford University Press, 1978.

162 Braubach, M., *Der Westfälishe Friede*, Münster, 1948.

163 Brightwell, P., 'The Spanish System and the Twelve Years Truce', in *English Historical Review*, no. 351, 1974.

164 Brightwell, P., 'Spain, Bohemia and Europe, 1619–21', in *European Studies Review*, vol. 12, no. 4, 1982.

165 Burckhardt, C. J., *Richelieu*, 3 vols., New York, 1964–72.

166 Cánovas del Castillo, A., *Estudios sobre el Reinado de Felipe IV*, 2 vols., Madrid, 1888–89.

167 Carsten, F. L., 'A Note on the Term "Thirty Years War"', in *History*, no. 149, 1958.

168 Carter, C. H., *The Secret Diplomacy of the Habsburgs, 1598–1625*, New York, 1964.

169 Church, W. F. *Richelieu and Raison d'Etat*, Princeton University Press, 1972.

170 Clasen, C. P., *The Palatinate in European History, 1555–1618*, Oxford, 1966.

171 Danstrap, J., *History of Denmark*, Copenhagen, 1948.

172 Dickens, A. G., *The Courts of Europe: Politics, Patronage and Royalty, 1400–1800*, Thames & Hudson, 1978.

173 Dickmann, F., *Der Westfälische Friede*, Stuttgart, 1965.

174 Elliott, J. H., 'The Statecraft of Olivares', in J. H. Elliott and H. G. Koenigsberger (eds.), *The Diversity of History*, Routledge & Kegan Paul, 1970.

175 Geyl, P., *The Netherlands Divided, 1609–48*, Williams & Norgate, 1936.

176 Green, M. A. E., *Elizabeth, Electress Palatine and Queen of*

Bohemia, London, 1909.

177 Hayden, J. M., *France and the Estates General of 1614*, Cambridge University Press, 1974.

178 Haywood, F., *Histoire de la Maison de Savoie*, Paris, 1943.

179 Jones, J. R., *Britain and Europe in the Seventeenth Century*, Arnold, 1966.

180 Kleinman, R., 'Charles Emmanuel I of Savoy and the Bohemian Election of 1619', in *European Studies Review*, V, 1975.

181 Koch, M., *Geschichte des deutschen Reiches unter der Refierung Ferdinands III*, vol. V, Leipzig, 1865–6.

182 Léonard, E., *A History of Protestantism, Volume II: The Establishment*, Nelson, 1967.

183 Lynch, J., *Spain under the Habsburgs*, vol. 2, Oxford, 1969.

184 Marañón, G., *El Conde-duque de Olivares*, Madrid, 1969.

185 Maltby, W., *The Black Legend in England: the Development of Anti-Spanish Sentiment 1558–1660*, Duke University Press, 1971.

186 Mecenseffy, G., 'Die Beziehungen der Höfe von Wien und Madrid Während des Dreissigjährigen Krieges', in *Archiv für Geschichte*, cxxi, 1953.

187 Oman, C., *Elizabeth of Bohemia*, London, 1938.

188 Parker, G., *Spain and the Netherlands 1559–1659: Ten Studies*, Fontana/ Collins, 1979.

189 Parker, G., *Philip II*, Hutchinson, 1979.

190 Quazza, R., *La guerra per la successione di Mantova e del Montferrata 1628–31*, 2 vols., Mantua, 1926.

191 Roberts, M., 'The Political Objectives of Gustavus Adolphus in Germany 1630–32', in *Transactions of the Royal Historical Society*, 1957.

192 Roberts, M., *Gustavus Adolphus: A History of Sweden 1611–32*. 2 vols., Longman, 1958.

193 Roberts, M., *Gustavus Adolphus and the Rise of Sweden*, Hodder & Stoughton, 1973.

194 Roberts, M., *The Swedish Imperial Experience*, Cambridge University Press, 1979.

195 Rudolf, H. U., (ed.), *Der Dreissigjährige Kreig: Perspektiven und Strukturen*, Darmstadt, 1977.

196 Schepper, H. de, and Parker, G., 'The Formation of Government Policy in the Catholic Netherlands under the Archdukes, 1596–1621', in *English Historical Review*, no. 359, 1976.

197 Schwarz, H. F., *The Imperial Privy Council in the Seventeenth*

Century, Cambridge, Mass., 1943.

198 Springell, F.C. (ed.), *Connoisseur and Diplomat: the Earl of Arundel's Embassy to Germany in 1636*, London, 1963.

199 Stolpe, S., *Christina of Sweden*, Burns & O.: A. Clarke Books, 1966.

200 Stradling, R., 'A Spanish Statesman of Appeasement: Medina de las Torres and Spanish Policy, 1630–70', in *Historical Journal*, vol. 19, 1976.

201 Stradling, R., *Europe and the Decline of Spain: A Study of the Spanish System 1580–1720*, Allen & Unwin, 1981.

202 Sturmberger, H., *Kaiser Ferdinand II und das Problem des Absolutismus*, Munich, 1957.

203 Tapié, V.L., *La Politique etrangère de la France et le début de la Guerre de Trente Ans 1616–21*, Paris, 1934.

204 Treasure, G.R.R., *Cardinal Richelieu and the Development of Absolutism*, Black, 1972.

205 Vilar, R.R., *La Política Europea de España durante la Guerra de Trente Años 1624–30*, Madrid, 1967.

206 Weber, H., *Frankreich, Kurtrier, der Rhein und das Reich, 1623–35*, Bornn, 1969.

207 Westin, G., *Negotiations about Church Unity 1628–34*, Upsala, 1932.

208 Wilson, C., *The Dutch Republic*, Weidenfeld & Nicolson, 1968.

209 Zeller, G., *La Guerre de Trente Ans et les relations internationales*, Paris, 1947.

RECENT PUBLICATIONS

210 Brightwell, P.J., 'The Spanish Origins of the Thirty Years War', in *European Studies Review*, 9, 1979, pp. 409–31.

211 Brightwell, P.J., 'Spain and Bohemia: the Decision to Intervene, 1619' in *European Studies Review*, 12, 1982, pp. 117–34.

212 Elliott, J.H., *Richelieu and Olivares*, Cambridge University Press, 1984.

213 Fernández-Santamaría, J.A., *Reason of State and Statecraft in Spanish Political Thought, 1595–1640*. Lanham, 1983.

214 Russell, Conrad, S.R., 'Monarchies, Wars and Estates in England, France, and Spain, c. 1580 – c.1640' in *Legislative Studies Quarterly*, 7, 1982, pp. 205–20.

215 Tomlinson, H. (ed.), *Before the English Civil War: Essays on Early Stuart Politics and Government*, Macmillan, 1983.

Index